DISCARD

*Political
Expectation*

PAUL TILLICH

Political
Expectation

HARPER & ROW,
PUBLISHERS

1817

NEW YORK, EVANSTON, SAN FRANCISCO, LONDON

The editor wishes to express warm appreciation here to Professor Victor Nuovo of Middlebury College for his conscientious assistance in the preparation of these translations for publication.

SOURCES OF ESSAYS IN Political Expectation

"Christianity and Modern Society," *The Student World (Geneva)*, XXI (1928), 282-90. Reprinted in *Gesammelte Werke (GW)* (Stuttgart: Evangelisches Verlagswerk, 1968), Vol. X.

"Protestantism as a Critical and Creative Principle," from *Protestantismus als Kritik und Gestaltung. Zweites Buch des Kairos-Kreises.* Ed., Paul Tillich (Darmstadt, 1929). Also, *GW* (1962), Vol. VII.

"Religious Socialism," under the title "Sozialismus: II. Religiöser Sozialismus," in *Die Religion in Geschichte und Gegenwart.* 2nd ed. (Tübingen, 1930), Vol. 5, pp. 637-48. Also, *GW* (1962), Vol. II.

"Basic Principles of Religious Socialism," under the title "Grundlinien des Religiösen Sozialismus," *Blatter für Religiosen Sozialismus*, IV, Heft 8/10 (1923). Also, *GW* (1962), Vol. II.

"Christianity and Marxism," in *Politische Studien. Monatschrift der Hochschule für Politische Wissenschaften* (Muenchen), XI, H. 119 (March, 1960), 149-54. Also in *Zeitwende. Die Neue Kirche*, XXXII, H. 1 (January, 1961), 24-29.

"The State as Expectation and Demand," in *Religiöse Verwirklichung* (Berlin, 1930). Also, *GW* (1967), Vol. IX.

"Shadow and Substance: A Theory of Power." Lecture delivered at the Graduate School of the Department of Agriculture, Washington, D.C., May 7, 1965.

"The Political Meaning of Utopia." Four lectures delivered at the Deutsche Hochschule für Politik, Berlin, in 1951. First published in the *Schriftenreihe der Deutschen Hochschule für Politik* (Berlin, 1953). Also, *GW* (1963), Vol. VI.

Contents

Introduction

JAMES LUTHER ADAMS

Most of the essays of the present volume were written in Germany more than forty years ago during the period of the Weimar Republic. Nevertheless, they speak to our contemporary condition, for the fundamental economic and political problems dealt with are still on the agenda in the United States as well as in other countries. In treating these problems from a Protestant perspective, Paul Tillich sets forth a constructive position which aims to interpret the structural maladjustments of "a late phase in the history of capitalism" and which endeavors also to uncover the grounds for hope, that is, for promise and "expectation." It should be noted, however, that the special essays on the latter theme—on what Ernst Bloch today calls "the impulse of expectation"—were written only two decades ago.

There is a second reason for the present significance of this volume. The theologians of the Weimar period are credited with having initiated a new period in the history of Protestant thought. Today the character and influence of these writings are being reassessed. The present volume represents a dimension of the earlier period which at that time and in our day has received less attention than that accorded to the more narrowly theological writings.

The period of the Weimar Republic was a time of severe social disruption, following upon a disastrous war of four years. During the war years Tillich served as a chaplain in the German army. In the Battle of Champagne in 1915 the experience of the whole period came for him, as it were proleptically, into a sharp focus of insight.

"It revealed to me," he says, "an abyss in human existence which could not be ignored." For him something more than a system of thought came into question. The abyss was the eruption of a social system. In this broad sense of protracted "emergency situation" was the smithy in which the ensuing essays were forged. A brief account of an all-night vigil held toward the end of the period will serve to evoke a vivid awareness of that situation.

In the summer of 1931, less than two years before the Nazis came to power, Paul and Hannah Tillich spent their vacation at Kampen, a resort on the large island of Sylt in the North Sea. One evening a group of friends were the guests of Mr. and Mrs. Günther Loewenfeld, all of them being from Berlin. Events were moving rapidly in Germany, and the group talked about them until dawn. Around four o'clock as the sun was rising they went out of the house to greet it and to look over the meadows down to the sea. As they stood there together Hannah Tillich quoted a poem by Goethe, about a ship at sea. Then there was silence again, each of them being absorbed in his own thoughts. Suddenly, Paul Tillich broke the silence. "And all of you," he said, "will live to see the day when sheep will graze in Potsdamer Platz." The prediction was verily a prologue to the omen coming on. . . . Years later, Tillich, living in New York City, to his astonishment read a news item from Germany showing that the prediction had come true. Sheep were grazing in Potsdamer Platz! Not only that. Potsdamer Platz had become a boundary between East and West Berlin.

This prediction had been uttered by a man who, with his associates in the Kairos Circle of religious socialists, had devoted persistent efforts for more than a decade to combat the forces that were now bringing on dark night and destruction. The failure of the Weimar Republic and of accompanying efforts at reform was becoming more and more clearly evident.

The forces that lay behind this failure are more or less familiar: the tensions growing out of the nationalistic and militarist ideologies in both liberal and conservative circles; the massive urban proletariat, and the acute division of the classes; the recalcitrance of the industrialists in face of the democratic idea and of parliamentary socialism; the adherence of the churches to the ruling groups, and the alienation of the workers from the churches; the disjunction between great industrial productive capacity and a restricted capacity for purchase in the market; the mounting unemployment; the jockeying for power of the Communists, the Social Democrats, and the Nationalists; the proved impossibility within the framework of the Republic for any soundly corrective group to gain power, especially in face of the great international Depression.

It is not surprising that even at the time of the founding of the Republic Oswald Spengler's *Decline of the West* with its prognosis of decay gained wide attention. Nor is it surprising that the men of the Kairos Circle, along with many others, believed that an old era of Western civilization was coming to an end.

In this situation Tillich, who had been somewhat active in politics and who was already developing a theology of culture, posed the question, What is the task of the theologian?[1] He knew full well that it was not to give the rhapsody of words belonging to sweet religion. It must bring every standpoint, including the "religious," under radical judgment and summon every standpoint to responsibility. He spoke of this thrust as "the vertical dimension" of a religious situation. At the same time he asserted that a religious situation is not confined to the sphere of "religion" as manifest in churches, creeds, liturgies. It embraces "the whole contemporary world, for there is nothing that is not in some way the expression of the religious situation."[2] This aspect he called "the horizontal dimension." An extremely important element in his theology of culture was the new vocabulary he devised in order to expose the situation and its possibilities with symbolic power. It is significant that this vocabulary was contrived in the midst of what he called "an emergency situation."[3]

[1] Cf. "On the Idea of a Theology of Culture" (1919) in James L. Adams (ed.), *What Is Religion?* (New York: Harper & Row, 1969).

[2] *The Religious Situation* (1925), tr. H. Richard Niebuhr (New York: Henry Holt & Co., 1932).

[3] We shall not here enumerate or define again the uniquely Tillichian vocabulary. See the present writer's *Paul Tillich's Philosophy of Culture, Science, and Religion* (Harper & Row, 1965; also Schocken Paperback, 1970); also "Tillich's Concept of the Protestant Era" in Paul Tillich, *The Protestant Era*, tr. and ed. James L. Adams (Chicago: The University of Chicago Press, 1948). Our intention here is rather to interpret some of the principal themes of the volume in relation to the *mise en scène* within which they originally appeared, and to refer to other writings of the author which deal with these themes.

We may bring into bold relief the range of Tillich's outlook if we contrast the scope of his response to the emergency situation with that of three of his influential contemporaries with whom he stood in close relationship, namely, Martin Heidegger, Rudolf Bultmann, and Karl Barth. By looking at these four men in their interrelations during the period of the Weimar Republic and by viewing three of them through the eyes of Tillich we shall be able in a special way to grasp Tillich's Religious Socialism in historical context. All four of these figures are often spoken of as existentialists. We cannot here discuss the question of the use and misuse of the term as applied to these four figures.

In Tillich's formulation, the significance of existentialism rests in its calling men back to Reality as immediately experienced and in its power to disclose again the questionable character of human existence (or "human being"), to see it in its contradictions, especially as they are manifest in our time, and thus to see it in its disruptedness, its abyss, its sense of meaninglessness and despair.

He identified two lines of existentialism, one line stemming from Kierkegaard and proceeding to Heidegger and Sartre, branching out (we might add) to include Bultmann and (in a limited way) Barth. Tillich affirmed his own affinities with this line, though he would add the name of Schelling to it as an initiator—we should recall here that Schelling coined the term *Existentialphilosophie*. But he saw himself to be related also to a second line, a prophetic line, that comes from Karl Marx and Friedrich Nietzsche, and beyond them from the Old Testament prophets. Here we should quote a striking passage in an important essay not included in the present volume. In this passage Tillich indicates that the second line of existentialism, like the first, includes ostensibly anti-religious as well as religious figures.

> In the nineteenth century the prophetic spirit broke forth in two places, and each time it was under the banner of a conflict with Christianity; in the case of Karl Marx and Friedrich Nietzsche. In Marx we find by word and deed the spirit of the old Jewish prophecy, and in Nietzsche the spirit of Luther. Although this battle, in the one case for justice and in the other for the creative life, took its form as a drive against God, it was an attack against

a God who had been bound to a standpoint, i.e., of bourgeois society.[4]

Equally important for Tillich, however, is a major difference between the two lines of existentialism. In the first line the understanding of existence is arrived at "by way of the existence of the individual," and in the second "by way of the historical-political situation." Tillich held that there is a "profound relationship" between the two lines.[5]

This affirmation of the profound relationship between the two lines is an illustration of Tillich's intention to live "on the boundary," a connecting as well as a separating link. In this connection he speaks of his theology of culture as a theology of mediation in the sense that it is an attempt "to define the way in which Christianity is related to secular culture." In his theology of culture there is scarcely a sphere of human concern which he does not deal with in a systematic way, but we shall confine attention here to the special concerns of the present volume, the areas of sociology, politics and economics. Heidegger, Bultmann and Barth, as we shall see, did not take seriously the demand for a broad theology of culture. Nor did they concern themselves in any continuing way with the concrete economic and political issues, despite their constant emphasis on the necessity for concreteness and decision (characteristic demands of existentialism). To be sure, Barth and Bultmann resisted Nazism after it came to power, at least a decade too late. But what they have to say in this respect has little bearing, except in a negative sense, on the unique problems of industrial society.

Tillich, however, often expressed strong appreciation for the three men under consideration. In an unpublished lecture on Heidegger, a one-time colleague on the faculty at Marburg, he speaks of him as "one of the great figures in the history of Western thought," a thinker "driven by the question of Being." Some of the ontological and much of the psychological language of the two men

4 "Ideen zur Geisteslage der Gegenwart," in *Kairos: Zur Geisteslage und Geisteswendung*, ed. Paul Tillich (Darmstadt, 1926), p. 4. Reprinted in *Gesammelte Werke* (Stuttgart, 1963), VI, 31. Hereafter this collected edition will be referred to as *GW*.

5 "Existentialism and Religious Socialism," *Christianity and Society*, XV, No. 1 (Winter, 1949-50), 8-9.

is identical or similar. This similarity bespeaks their possession of a common philosophical background, though Heidegger considered himself an atheist, a person lacking in religious faith.

In contrast to Tillich's existentialism Heidegger's is arrived at only "by way of the individual," and he seeks only to define the authenticity of individual existence. Authentic existence overcomes man's "forgetfulness of Being" and his alienation from Reality. Authenticity is interpreted in terms of self-relatedness or in interpersonal terms, and not in institutional terms. Tillich speaks of "an atheistic sermon" which Heidegger "once gave to us in his pietistic categories." Reporting a conversation with Heidegger, he tells us that in saying this to him he had in mind the pietistic homiletical language he had heard in his youth. He could also refer to the language reminiscent of Kierkegaardian psychological terms (such as anxiety, despair, dread) used by Heidegger in order to "enter into the mystery of Being," and to bring men back to Reality.

Heidegger's concern with the individual in authentic relation to Being, determines the definition of all of his characteristic concepts. For example, the concept of historicity is defined in such a way as to center attention on the need of the individual to free himself from the inauthenticity induced by social-institutional forces (especially a technological society) and from the conventionalities of Everyman. In authentic historicity the individual becomes a "subject" escaping from the imprisonment of being a mere "object thrown into a world of objects," and opens himself resolutely to the future, to newness of life. This is a severely truncated, Gnostic conception of "the historical," centering in an abstract voluntaristic act. As Tillich puts it, Heidegger's "abstract use of the concept of 'the historical' obscures the concrete historical conditioning of his thought."[6] In his essay in the present volume on "Historical and Unhistorical Thinking" he says it is "the very negation of every concrete relation to history . . . Heidegger has abstracted man from all real history." Indeed, we may say that Heidegger in his exclusive attention to individual psychology and ontology employs an efficient means of avoiding any responsible or systematic concern for the

---

6 "Die Theologie des Kairos und die gegenwärtige geistige Lage," *Theologische Blätter*, XXIII, No. 11 (November, 1934), 316.

realities and responsibilities of the socio-political order.[7] Something analogous to this must be said of Bultmann.

Tillich held Bultmann in high esteem as a New Testament scholar of remarkable integrity and independence of judgment, though he was critical in certain ways of his method of demythologizing religious symbols. The Marburg theologian makes it clear from the outset that his approach is strictly by way of the individual. Already in 1920 he asserts that "the meaning of religion is the being, the life, of the individual."[8] With Bultmann, as with Heidegger, the subject-object schema plays a central role, for the ultimate resources of authentic existence are held to be beyond this cleavage. But unlike Heidegger, Bultmann makes the schema decisive for the understanding of religion. Only through the grace of God (an unobjectified God) is man liberated from confinement in the capsule of objectivity. Religion is sharply distinguished from culture. Following the Marburg Neo-Kantians, Bultmann considers the spheres of culture—science, art, morality and the political order—to be spheres of creativity where the human spirit becomes objectified. Revealing also his Lutheran orientation, he interprets all of these objectifying activities as "works" wherein universality, necessity and supra-individual laws obtain. But authentic religion, subsisting only in the inner life of the unique individual, is not a cultural force, nor is it to be understood as a form of creativity or of "works." Since it depends upon the gift of grace, the man of faith responds in absolute passivity and self-abandon. This is the pith and marrow of man's

7 But even within the confines of Heidegger's individualism Tillich observes a radical deficiency. Heidegger, he says, "has no norms, no criteria, for his 'resolute-ness.' It remains without direction." This lack of norms, he continues, explains why Heidegger was willing to collaborate for a time with the Nazis and to become the Nazi rector of the University of Freiburg. "There he suddenly had a lot of resoluteness, more than he could find before anywhere. But this resolute-ness was . . . demonic." In discussing Heidegger's collaboration with the Nazis, Tillich shows himself to be charitable in judgment. "You cannot judge a philoso-pher," he says, "in terms of his shortcomings in life. . . . The fact that Plato was foolish enough to become the adviser of the Hitler of his time, the tyrant of Syracuse, shows that you cannot identify a philosopher with his personal de-cisions." Quotations from "Heidegger and Jaspers," an unpublished lecture delivered at the Cooper Union Forum, New York City, March 23, 1954, p. 6.

8 "Religion and Culture," tr. L. DeGrazia and K. R. Crim, in James M. Robinson (ed.), *The Beginnings of Dialectical Theology* (Richmond, Va.: John Knox Press, 1968), p. 211.

attribute under God. There can therefore be no history of authentic religion. Real history takes place only in the life of the individual, giving rise to trust, friendship and love. Authentic historicity appears only in awareness of the concrete situation in its possibilities for "the new." The I-Thou relatonship is the authentic and productive relationship. In his (dubious) interpretation of the New Testament message, Bultmann presents the preaching of Jesus as "directed not primarily to the people as a whole but to individuals. . . . Thus, Jesus in his thought of God—and of man in the light of this thought —'de-historized' God and man."[9] Bultmann accordingly de-historizes revelation, history, and the kingdom of God—and even the future in general. For this reason Tillich in an unpublished lecture on Bultmann speaks of his being "accused of bringing everything into the experience and decision of the individual."

The emphasis of Bultmann is conducive in the main to the privatization of piety. Apart from his heroic Marburg lecture at the advent of the Nazi regime it is difficult to find discussion in his writings of the "emergency situation" of the Weimar Republic, of the "abyss" in the historical situation of which Tillich speaks. To be sure, as a consequence of his resistance to the Nazis he suffered harassment at their hands; and as a leader in the confessing church he (and his family) lived in constant anxiety. Yet, one must say that his notion of authenticity is in the main a transcendentalized subjectivity, a highly organized withdrawal from history. It is a spatialized authenticity, an idolatry, of the inner life and of interpersonal relations, by default an adjustment to the objective world of social-institutional existence. Accordingly, Jürgen Moltmann asks of Bultmann the question, "Is any self-understanding of man conceivable at all which is not determined by his relation to the world, to history, to society?"[10] Tillich would add the question, Is Bultmann's kind of self-understanding possible without the attendant support of a social order? Bultmann's theology presupposes a stable society, a pietistic bourgeois existence with a regular paycheck, everyone minding his own vocational business, always open

---

9 *Theology of the New Testament*, tr. Kendrick Grobel (New York: Charles Scribner's Sons, 1951), I, 25.

10 *Theology of Hope*, tr. James W. Leitsch (New York: Harper & Row, 1965), p. 65.

to spontaneous, concrete decision for the neighbor—surely false securities.

In face of the pervasive social, economic and political realities and responsibilities, in face of the massive, demonic forces that harrow up the soul, Heidegger and Bultmann offer pietistic escape from history, estrangement from civil authenticity. Their concern is primarily with the vertical to the neglect of the horizontal, civic dimension, "the historical-political situation." In reality, however, their concern in its effect is what Tillich repeatedly speaks of as ideology—a concealed defense of the status quo so long as it does not disturb inner and individual freedom.

The assessment of Bultmann is obviously not intended as an estimate of his contribution as an outstanding New Testament scholar or as a "demythologizer." It is confined to a consideration of his doctrine of man and society and of his conception of historicity. Similarly limited must be the brief consideration here of Karl Barth.

Tillich, from the beginning days of dialectical theology and always thereafter, expressed profound appreciation for Barth's "mighty proclamation." For him, Barth's protest against Culture-Protestantism was a bolt from heaven. In his first critical article on dialectical theology (1923) he said that "everything must be done to make the cutting edge of this criticism felt in wide circles . . ."[11] He then went on to say, however, that Barth's God was something less than unconditional, indeed that it approached being an objectified reality, a demonic negation—judgment without grace. We cannot here recount this particular debate, the reply and the rejoinder, a debate in which Barth spoke of Tillich's critique as "presumptuous." In those days Barth was anything but mellow or receptive to criticism.

Almost a decade earlier Barth had associated himself with the Swiss Religious Socialist movement, especially with the ideas of the younger Blumbhardt and Hermann Kutter; and before the First World War he had joined the Social Democratic Party. What with this background and what with his emphasis on objective revelation and his devastating criticism of "religious experience," he was cer-

[11] James M. Robinson (ed.), *op. cit.*, p. 133.

tainly no pietist; moreover, not long after his theological movement
was launched he insisted that his theology in no way depended upon
existential philosophy. Despite his earlier religious-socialist commitment, however, he abandoned his concern for the historical-political
situation. In Tillich's view, Barth's change of direction was due to
the fact that his theology was not really dialectical, especially by
reason of his radical separation between God and the world, between religion and ethics, and between the Kingdom of God and
history. He had lost the sense of the paradoxical immanence of the
transcendent. Tillich speaks of this fundamental aspect of Barth's
theology as "undialectical supernaturalism," thus anticipating
Dietrich Bonhoeffer's later characterization of it as "revelation
positivism." He held that this dualism (which appeared even to
derogate the doctrine of creation) weakened Barth's prophetic power,
particularly because of its abstract and indiscriminate criticism of
all cultural phenomena. Barth had been concretely critical of both
liberal and orthodox theology. But his dualism carried him away
from specificity of criticism of the socio-political situation (until after
Nazism was already in power). In 1926 Tillich wrote:

> It ["so-called dialectical theology"] remains consciously remote
> in an abstract "No" against the time, and it does not become con-
> cretely critical of the time. . . . Since it remains in the abstract
> "No," it does not know a concrete "No." This would not be so
> serious if the renunciation of a concrete "No" were not in its effect
> a concrete "Yes" to the status quo. Thus for the present time it is
> a virtual support of bourgeois society and an obstruction to the
> spiritual forces struggling against that spirit.[12]

The Kairos Circle therefore looked upon Barth as an escapist in
the name of an extravagantly transcendent God. Tillich, at that
time and later on, spoke of the devastating effects of Barth's theology
on movements like Religious Socialism (which tried to strengthen
German democratic socialism) as well as on its spiritual power to
resist the threat of National Socialism. Barth's withdrawal from
history "prevented many from seeing the religious issue involved in
the political situation of post-war Germany," and he did this by

12 "Ideen zur Geisteslage der Gegenwart," *op. cit., GW,* VI, 32.

"the strict separation of history from super-history."[13] Tillich for his part found little comfort in Barth's claim that he maintained "subterranean connection" with Religious Socialism. Barth allowed undialectical concern for the vertical dimension to crowd out concrete concern for the horizontal dimension; he also allowed abstract prophetic criticism to crowd out rational criticism. This view is set forth extensively below in the essay on "Protestantism as a Critical and Creative Principle," where at the same time Barth's remoteness from concrete social realities is compared to the abstract type of criticism stemming from Kant.

Before the First World War, Tillich was, as he puts it, "rather indifferent to politics." Before the war he had been writing on Schelling and on supernaturalist theology prior to Schleiermacher. Because of the revolution of the last year of the war, however, he "began to understand" such issues as the political background of the war, the interrelation between capitalism and imperialism, and the crisis of bourgeois society. Before long he became a member of the Independent Social Democratic Party (the left wing), and then formed the Kairos Circle which in 1920 began to publish a magazine. Among some of his colleagues he was spoken of as a "Red Socialist." In 1919 (when he was thirty-three) the Protestant Consistory of Brandenburg directed an inquiry to him, asking him to justify his membership and activity in a party that was vigorously anti-religious. The situation reminds one of the time twenty years before this when the pastor Christoph Blumhardt was constrained to write a letter to his associates in the churches to explain to them his having joined the Social Democratic Party (he was elected in the same year to represent the Party in the provincial legislature). Tillich, in his response, gave, among other things, the substance of a lecture he had

---

13 "Karl Barth's Turning Point," review of *The Church and the Political Problem of Our Day, Christendom,* V (1940), 129-31. In this book review Tillich says that "whether Barth himself admit it or not (probably he would not), this book means a turning point in his theology," for the book implies that "the demand for a theological interpretation and judgment of politics generally" is entailed "as Religious Socialism always had demanded." Of Barth's outlook in the 1920's, we may recall here, Reinhold Niebuhr was wont to speak of as "quietism" amounting to "sanctified futilitarianism." He wrote numerous articles in this vein in *The Christian Century.*

previously delivered at the invitation of the Party. On the one hand, he rejects every attempt to identify Christianity with any particular social order and thus to deprive religion of its inward personal character. On the other hand, he asserts that Christianity carries within it the power and the will to shape the life of humanity in its own terms; and therefore he rejects every form of Christianity which wishes to adhere only to pure inwardness. He then proceeds to set forth many of the ideas he developed in theological elaboration in the succeeding years. Probably Professor and Mrs. Wilhelm Pauck in their forthcoming biography will present in some detail the circumstances and the other ideas of this extraordinary statement, a statement that is constructively critical of both the Party and the churches.

What lay behind this dual criticism was the conviction that a spiritual cleavage in the life of the individual is always related to social and political, and especially to economic, cleavage, and that neither cleavage is properly confronted in separtion from the other. Accordingly, Tillich allied himself with both lines of existentialism, toward the end of defining individual and social authenticity in their relatedness.[14] Both types of existentialism disclose the tensions and contradictions, the abyss of meaninglessness and despair in our present existence, thus exposing its inauthenticity. Here the subject-object schema becomes significant in two ways: the conception of individual and social authenticity demands a transformation of society wherein "every group and every individual can find the meaning of life, and in which the present demonries are provisionally mitigated . . ."[15] In this new freedom the subject may relate himself to the actual and latent meaning of the objective world. But then the question arises as to the source and resource for any such thrust in history.

Existentialism has been correct in raising the question regarding source and resource. But no existentialism as such can give an

---

[14] Tillich did not himself always keep the two lines in tension with each other after he had lost his home-base in Germany. Much of his writing on depth psychology and psychotherapy seems to have been in response to the popularity of the first line of existentialism "by way of the individual." He even tended to "spiritualize" the second line of existentialism.

[15] "Religiöser Sozialismus," *Neue Blätter für den Sozialismus*, I (1930), 402-403; *GW*, II, 158.

answer. In existentialism, then, Tillich finds predicament and
question, and attempts to present a Christian answer. (Later on he
will call this "the method of correlation.") The answer he proposes
combines ontological, theological and ethical elements.[16] The demand for a new spirit and meaning requires that men (and groups)
shall open themselves to a power that transcends both subject and
object, the ultimate source of both judgment and grace, the source
also of an enkindling eschatological lure. Already in 1915 Tillich
was saying that God is not "a being beside other beings," and he was
speaking of the "God beyond God."

One of the least authentic responses to the question and to "the
religious situation" is the response that attempts to de-historize
history and expectation. In face of the multiple forms of the
privatization of piety and responsibility the problem of our period
is that of re-historizing history, and of recapturing the eschatological
passion which has largely faded out of Christianity and which is
alive in Marxism. Accordingly, in the essays below on "The Political
Significance of Utopia" Tillich sets forth a typology of conceptions
of history and expectation, toward the end of adumbrating a
"dynamic" and "dialectical" eschatology.

If now we turn more particularly to the horizontal dimension of
history, we against encounter dialectic. Every living form, Tillich
says, contains in its depth the conflict between a present and a
becoming form. We proceed from the intuition of a becoming form
and from the conflict into which it drives the existing form. The
danger, however, is that the expectation will turn out to be utopian
in the sense that it does not reckon with the demands and the
possible perversions of the organization of power. Yet, it is equally
unrealistic to suppose that a way out and forward may be taken
without risk. One thing is especially clear, that history is made
by moving from where we are, by latching onto what is. Dialectic
looks to reality and to the trends inherent in it, and places itself in
the service of the critical and creative trends, under the impulse of
the Kairos.

The sense of Kairos is twofold: at the right time, the time to be

16 In this connection see "The Interpretation of History and the Idea of Christ"
(1929), in *Interpretation of History*, tr. N. A. Rasetzki and Elsa L. Talmey (New
York: Charles Scribner's Sons, 1936).

taken by the forelock, it perceives the becoming form as the fulfillment of a divinely given, immediately relevant possibility; and it
guards against absolutizing any envisaged possibility. Here we see
Tillich's application of "the Protestant principle" to the temporal,
historical process. (It is curious to observe, however, that he seldom
addresses himself explicitly to questions of strategy regarding the
ways in which a social movement may acquire or share power in
its effort to gain a toe-hold in history. Is this because he assumes
that history is made by linking onto powers that are already in gear?)

In the light of these criteria the American reader will perhaps
be surprised that Tillich in the 1920's seemed to believe that
Protestantism should see promise in an alliance with Marxism. In
actuality, such a notion was far from his purpose. Instead, he conceived of each as offering something fundamental to the other.
Initially, he was struck by the insight of Christoph Blumhardt that
at certain times the thrust of the Kingdom of God could be found to
a greater degree in Social Democracy (though it was opposed to
religion and the church) than in the official representatives of
religion. Proceeding from this insight, he came to the view that by
being critical of both Social Democracy and the churches one might
find a connection and even a unity in principle between them. After
all, both Protestantism and Social Democracy were in process of
development (there is no such thing as a ready-made religion or a
read-made socialism), and if one examined them to their roots
(ideological taints and all), one might uncover hidden or latent
authenticities; and self-correction of demonic elements in both
might become possible. He could make such a proposal because he
was convinced that Marxism with its ethical passion and eschatological fire is not understandable apart from its connection with
Christian humanism and Old Testament prophetism. Taken together, the writings of Tillich on this theme are more elaborate
and systematic than anything else available.

Tillich in recent decades often insisted, however, that the Neo-
Marxist formulations of Religious Socialism did not fit the American
scene, indeed that the expectations entertained for the Weimar
Republic were unrealistically utopian. As a consequence of his
experience in the United States he acknowledged that the theory of
the planned society with centralized governmental power was not

"in the cards" for American development (though he saw many features of socialism being adopted by the welfare state). Instead, he came to believe in the necessity and rightness of a dispersion of power in a mixed economy. This view becomes evident if one examines the concluding document of the present volume. Tillich also came to see similarities as well as dissimilarities between Religious Socialism and the American Social Gospel, and along with Reinhold Niebuhr he contributed to its transformation.[17]

It is noteworthy, however, that in his later years Tillich in his treatment of "political expectation" came to the view that in the current period we are at a sort of stalemate, indeed that we are living in a "sacred void," and that we must wait in hope. Demonically "possessed" by our national arrogance, we have "too many illusions about our own goodness and distortions of the image of others."[18] Yet, he who waits in absolute seriousness is always grasped by that for which he waits—the power of transformation.

A century and a half ago William Ellery Channing, on hearing an advocate of the use of the lash in the army, the navy, and the prisons, broke forth with, "What! Strike a *man!*" A long period of time was required to bring this practice more generally into disrepute. An equally long period of time has been required for America to awaken to poverty (and unemployment and racism) as a social problem and as a common responsibility. Even today ten million citizens in the United States are in "food jeopardy," largely because local authorities wish them to remain hungry as a "punishment for their indolence"! The late Bishop Francis J. McConnell used to say (in American idiom), "The trouble is not that we don't get mad but that we don't stay mad."

The essays of the present volume will long remain a potent resource in the human venture, for they demonstrate the thesis that authentic "political expectation" must be accompanied by a "political theology" that is at the same time realistic, critical and boldly creative—nourished by the substance of things hoped for.

17 "Between Utopianism and Escape from History," *Colgate Rochester Divinity School Bulletin*, XXXI, No. 2 (May, 1959). A Rauschenbusch Lecture.
18 "The Right to Hope," *Neue Zeitschrift für systematische Theologie und Religionsphilosophie*, VII, Heft 3 (1965), 375.

Christianity and Modern Society*

An inquiry into the relationship of Christianity and modern
society necessitates the answer to a prior question: namely, what is
the standpoint of the question and its answer? This question immediately reveals the great difficulty of the undertaking. To answer
"from the standpoint of Christianity" presupposes that one could,
if he would, take a Christian standpoint beyond modern society.
To answer "from the standpoint of modern society" presupposes
that there is a position alongside Christianity. Both presuppositions
are false. No one can have Christianity apart from modern society
in which he lives, which has borne him, and formed him with its
language, its institutions, and its people. Even if he should strive
passionately to free himself from his native environment he would
not succeed, not even for a moment. If he wanted to base his life
exclusively on the Bible or the doctrines of the ancient church,
every word that he read would inadvertently be colored by his
understanding, that is, ultimately, by the life and language of
modern society. No one can escape from himself. We are, for the
most part, the modern society in which we live. There is no standpoint for us apart from modern society. But just as little can there
be a modern standpoint apart from Christianity. No one living in
the modern world can free himself from Christianity. It has per-
meated all the institutions and customs of modern society, as well
as its morality and intellectual life (*Geistesleben*). One can become
secular, but not "pagan." For "pagan" is a religious concept that

* Translated by John C. Modschiedler; revised in part by Victor Nuovo.

has been destroyed by Christianity, which because of Christianity can no longer be held in good conscience, and which Christianity has revealed as demonic. The standpoint of modern society is not a standpoint apart from Christianity.

Whenever we speak of the relationship of Christianity and modern society we therefore can do so only as persons who occupy both positions, whose standpoint intersects both. We who ask and answer questions are products of the cooperation of both Christianity and modern society, and it is impossible for anyone to separate the different elements that form this unity. This means that when we ask about the relationship of Christianity and modern society, we are asking a concrete question, indeed, the question that concerns our concrete existence. Furthermore, it signifies that we cannot answer it from a standpoint that is outside our own existence, outside Christianity and modern society. Every answer that we can give here is a struggle for our own situation, a leap from our own present into the future. It has the seriousness of risk. The question of the relationship of Christianity and modern society has meaning not as an academic investigation of something in which we take no part, but as an act in which we are ourselves involved.

The answer to this question must necessarily take into account the relationship between these two important factors in the history of ideas. It will therefore involve a substantiation and elaboration of our introductory remarks. Christianity is the background of modern society in its religious substance—Christianity in general and Protestant Christianity in particular. Behind all the thought and life of modern society stands the Judaeo-Christian victory over the pagan-demonic attitude toward the world. Belief in creation includes the belief that matter, even earthly matter, is not something opposed to God. As God's creation it is perfect on all stages of its development. Therefore, it is not necessary to flee from matter in order to reach God. A resounding Yes is pronounced upon the entire creation. The Yes of the Renaissance to the earth, the lifting up of the earth to the realm of the stars, the assertion that the divine essense is no nearer to the realm of the stars than to the earth, that it is present everywhere—this is the profound truth of the Christian doctrine of creation. It stands in contradiction, theoretically and practically, to that attitude toward life which prevailed throughout antiquity. Moreover, Christian monotheism implies that the world is not ruled by various divine powers and, therefore, is basically divided and demonic, rather the world has a unitary meaning, a unitary origin and goal. The divine is a spiritual and moral unity, and the world is the place destined for its dominion. The faith of the Renaissance in the earth as a place of meaningful creative activity, and the promise of a reign of righteousness and humaneness which resounded in the utopian schemes of that age, do not come from antiquity but from Christianity. Although it appeared as if the old gods had returned, it was not the gods themselves who came but their power which was incorporated in the one moral God who was free from all demonic disunity. Gods do not die, but neither do they return. They are transformed and enter into the true God. It is not the gods of antiquity who ruled the Renaissance and modern society, but the one God to whom Christianity bears witness.

In addition to this more remote, often neglected background of modern society there is the more familiar and much discussed Protestant background. Modern society became possible primarily through Protestanism. It is indebted to it for the concept of personality and for the sanctification of daily life. Sacramental and hierarchical religion broke down before the onslaught of the individual conscience wrestling with God—conscience which no one and nothing, neither sacred reality nor a "form of grace," could deprive of its responsibility. All sacred realms and all sacramental and ascetic works lose their value in face of the daily practice of obedience. Both ideas have found their way into modern society in many and diverse forms.

The ideal of individual personality can be interpreted either as subjective piety—as in Pietism and Methodism—or as the subjection of the sinner to judgment and grace—as in orthodox Protestantism. And the sanctification of daily life can be a sanctification of the status quo [the existing social order[1]]—as on Lutheran soil—or a sanctification of the process of transformation [of society]—as on Reformed soil. In either case, however, it is always a typically Protestant spirit that manifests itself therein. And modern society

[1] Translator's additions in this chapter are in brackets.

bears this spirit in one form or another, whether it knows it or not.
Of course, this is all background. The foreground is quite another
matter. All that we have discussed is the substance of modern society
—the substance upon which it lives to this day, but the form of that
substance exists no longer. A new factor has been added: the
secularization, the desecration, and the transformation into sheer
this worldliness of the religious heritage. Modern society is secular.
Its affections dwell upon the this-worldly for the sake of the this-
wordly. As I expressed it earlier in *The Religious Situation,* modern
society is "self-sufficient finitude."[2] The religious personalities of
both forms [of Society] have become secular personality types, either
humanistic or romantic; and the sanctification of daily life has been
replaced by the commonplace. The acceptance of creation and the
world has become worldiness, and the will to religious transformation of the world has become autonomous politics, economics, and
technology. The Protestant Christian background for each of these
developments may be shown, yet each has also torn itself away from
its background. Modern society is the autonomous and secular phase
of Protestant Christian society. Therein unity and contrast are combined. Therein lies the basis for the utter uncertainty in the stance
of each toward the other: vacillation between affirmation and denial,
between identification and opposition.

Christianity cannot avoid recognizing itself in modern society; at
the same time, however, it must see modern society as the locus of
all opposition to Christianity. And in spite of all its protests
against the churches' threat to its autonomy, modern society piously
continues to acknowledge the Christian substance of society as its
own. Out of this situation comes the manifold intricacies, the very
rich interplay, of both these magnitudes, which in turn can be
understood only when one recognizes the situation. Whereas
the early church was faced with a pagan society in religious and
secular forms, and the medieval church existed alongside a substantially pagan but culturally Christian society, the modern church
stands simultaneously in union and in tension with a substantially
Christian but culturally secular society (cf. Eugen Rosenstock and
Josef Wittig, *Das Alter der Kirche,* Berlin, 1927). The result of this

---

2 "In sich ruhende Endlichkeit"; the translation is H. Richard Niebuhr's.

state of affairs has been twofold: on the one hand, the assimilation of the churches into the creations of modern, secular society, and, on the other hand, a faint protest against modern society from the standpoint of older intellectual and social forms.

The historical destiny of the various forms of Protestantism led each to very different solutions to this general situation. In Lutheran circles the relation to the *intellectual* life of modern society stood in the foreground; in Calvinist circles it was the relation to *social* life. In Lutheran-influenced culture, the church chose to deal with philosophical and literary questions; in culture under Calvinism's influence the choice fell upon political and social questions. Naturally, this contrast is not without exception. The fact that intellectual reflection was thrust into the foreground of Lutheranism was connected with the structure of society in the Lutheran state churches. That the socio-economic structure of society was decisive for Calvinism is also accounted for in the basic solution of its intellectual problems.

In Anglo-American culture the solution to the problem of knowledge is basically conservative. Autonomous science and philosophy have their own position. On the whole, a desire for mutual adjustment is lacking. God is banished to the outer limits of philosophic thought without his having any influence upon it. Ethics is based on the principle of utility, but it lives on contents which are the remainder of a Christian ethos and for whose secularized reinterpretation the concept of altruism is typical. The transformation of society is undertaken with all the more energy. In the name of Christianity the English revolution created a capitalist society as the realization of the rule of God. In religion and in the formal structuring of life all the demonically ecstatic elements of feudal times were suppressed. The Bible became the law book of the people. Even the monarchy was obliged to subject itself to it. The heroic personality which rests upon the belief in predestination subjects itself to the world, which itself is subject to the discipline of the divine law. But heroism is no durable mein; it is the possibility of a social stratum in a historical moment. Then it becomes custom and law. Thus did the manner of living of capitalist society come about. Religion was transformed into the economic and technical mastery of the world, into humanitarianism and the worldly development of personality. The religious background was preserved. To this day it may not be impugned. Its unshakenness in the intellectual and epistemological sphere sees to that. Nevertheless, it slides imperceptibly into the secular, which tacitly and all the more naturally prevails. And with secularization the shaping of Christianity falls into the hands of the supporting forces of capitalist society—the economic and the political. Assimilation into the forms of life of the economically dominant bourgeoisie, and subordination to the political unity of the dominant Anglo-Saxon capitalist state became equated with assimilation into theocracy. And this also occurs with all the more effectiveness whenever it happens inadvertently. As a result, however, Christianity's standpoint for possible opposition to capitalist society has disappeared. Christianity and modern society have been brought to the point of identity.

Therefore, Western Protestantism leaves autonomous culture untouched in the realm of knowledge, but also preserves untouched its own dogmatic fundamentals, in the social realm it creates capitalist society with which it identifies. From both standpoints, however, a critical opposition to modern society has become impossible.

In lands with churches of Lutheran orientation the entire intellectual development was directly determined by Christianity. In the German classic and romantic periods the idea of God was always the root problem. The struggle for a "theonomous" culture permeates all of German philosophy. And contrariwise, the transforming forces of philosophy and literature constantly enter into theology and change all the symbols of religious knowledge. This is the battleground and sphere of accommodation between Christianity and modern society. For some time it appeared as though Christianity would be absorbed by the forms thus created—as though an identification of Christianity with German Idealism would occur. But this danger was basically overcome as a result of the breakdown of Idealism in the nineteenth century. Then the opposite danger arose: the separation of religion and knowledge in the manner of Western Protestantism. Since the turn of the century this danger, too, has been overcome. Now we are in the midst of a most lively and mutually fruitful harmony and opposition on the part of Christian and autonomous intellectual life. The hidden goal thereby is in each case "theonomy," that is, Christian fulfillment of autonomous forms.

In the social and political sphere, however, the case was quite different. Here the actively revolutionary society was not the bearer of Protestant forms, as had been the case in the West but, rather, the system of local princedoms. Because of the doctrine that made the local prince the highest-ranking bishop, the position of prince received religious sanction. Because of Luther's doctrine of the divine institution of civil authority, even when that authority was unchristian in character, every possible configuration in opposition to the state was forbidden. The Protestant churches became a department of public administration. The capitalist revolution of the nineteenth century no longer had any religious significance; it was disavowed by the churches. Later, an attempt was made to divert the proletarian movement and incorporate it into the patriarchal-princely system of government and at the same time to win the movement for Christianity and the monarchy. When that failed, it too was just as sharply and even more bitterly attacked than the capitalist revolution, with whose effects in the meantime they had in some measure come to terms. Nevertheless, this acquiescence to certain changes on the part of the ruling classes was not complete. A silent protest against modern capitalist society was always maintained. It emanated from the petty-bourgeois feudal structure of the Lutheran state churches and from Christianity's alliance with the precapitalist social order. With the collapse of the monarchy and the princedoms this silent protest lost any opportunity it may have had to establish itself politically. After the revolution it linked itself with those parties in which the old conservative elements were most clearly preserved. In this way the intimate connection between the Lutheran Church and the German National Party came about, even though it was officially denied. But the protest that arises against modern society from these quarters is powerless, because it is made in the name of a basically obsolete social structure. It does not arise out of the center of the present social scene. And as a result of the intimate political connections between the conservative circles and the economically dominant middle class, the anticapitalist protest has the singular effect of being a campaign against the socialist movement. It is almost impossible for a proletarian to perceive the anticapitalist, Christian element in the conservatism, say, of younger intellectuals. The resolute political opposition to the proletariat on the part of the conservative parties is all too evident. The result is that Christianity's influence upon socio-political developments and forms is extremely slight. Only in the fringe areas of capitalist society—in the peasant class, among middle-class bureaucrats and the petty bourgeoisie—can any effects of Christianity be seen. These effects, however, are chiefly conservative in character and for that reason are completely uncreative.

These facts, in turn, are not without import for the intellectual sphere. The danger becomes ever greater that wide circles of the Evangelical Church will fall prey to an ideology that no longer has anything to do with the actual structure of society. Intellectual and spiritual life, no matter how vital it may be, is doomed to fruitlessness and emptiness if it does not receive new impulses from the actual social situation and the challenge which it presents. Religious socialism makes the exceedingly difficult attempt, on both the intellectual and the social level, to work toward a form of future society in which the autonomous life of that society will be filled with the meaning-giving essence of Christianity. Whether this attempt will be successful in the face of stiffening opposition and under the weight of the reality of the capitalistic middle-class socio-economic order is highly questionable. Nevertheless, the attempt must be made. It is—as far as I can see—the only movement that attacks the problem, "Christianity and modern society," where it must be attacked, namely, at the point of greatest social tension: the conflict between the middle class and the proletariat.

But, of course, religious socialism—even if it were more powerful and effective than it actually is—cannot create what is prerequisite for a truly vital relationship between Christianity and modern society, namely, the visible presence of Christian "being," the "form of grace." (Concerning this concept, see my essay, "Protestantism as a Critical and Creative Principle," pp. 10-40.) This is what gives Catholicism an advantage over Protestantism: it has such a form of grace which is present and visible, even if it has become demonic. Hence, its relationship to modern society is much easier to determine, but it also has less depth and is less fruitful; for Catholicism represents a form of grace which Protestantism, with irrevocable historical force, has pushed into the past. Catholicism is incapable of offering a solution to the present social problem. However, in relation to Protestantism, Catholicism makes one thing clear: where a visible form of grace is lacking, religious life becomes subject to political and social forces and cannot avoid secularization. It vacillates between uncreative protest and naïve identification. There can be a solution to the problem of "Christianity and modern society" only where and to the extent that a form of grace exists visibly in reality—not paralyzed and not authoritarian, as in Catholicism, but pointing beyond the human limits of society and at the same time participating in culture's autonomous struggle.

Thus, it has not been given to us to set forth a general solution to the problem; rather, we have the task of working at every single point toward a new "form of grace" which stands in the midst of modern society as its judge, its true meaning, and the indication of its fulfillment. The more deeply we share in our historical moment, and the more fully we enter into the tensions between Christianity and modern society, the sooner will that which is independent of our choosing be accomplished through us: the coming of a "form of grace" in which Christianity and the society of the future have entered into a new relationship.

Protestantism as a Critical and Creative Principle*

1. PROTESTANTISM AS A CRITICAL PRINCIPLE

a. The Two Types of Criticism

The criticism of intellectual and social forms may proceed from two different points of view. The one is the standpoint of the ideal by which the particular form is measured. The other standpoint is that which lies beyond the creation of form.[1] From the latter point of view form-creation as such is brought into question. The first type of criticism presupposes a definite standard by means of which it is able to pronounce its Yes or its No. It is a rational procedure, even though the criterion itself has not been reached in a rational way. The second kind of criticism possesses no criterion at all; for that which lies beyond form-creation is not a form that can be used for the measurement of other forms. Therefore, it does not pronounce a Yes or a No, but combines an unconditioned No with an unconditioned Yes. This type of criticism is not rational but prophetic.[2] Thus, for example, any scientific result is measured by that

---

* Translated by James L. Adams; revised by Victor Nuovo.

[1] The German word *Gestalt* is here rendered by the word "form," and the word *Gestaltung* is rendered "creative and formative power" and "form-creation." (Tr.)

[2] The term "prophetic" is abstracted from the unique phenomenon of Hebrew prophecy; thus it signifies a proclaiming of the crisis in which all life stands, coming from "beyond all life." Such an abstraction would be justifiable for critical theological research (*Wissenschaft*) even if Hebrew prophecy were to be interpreted as unique in a strictly supernatural sense.

standard of scientific evidence which is valid in the particular field in question. However, the structure of science as such is brought into question—and perhaps justified—by what is beyond all human knowledge, by what is "higher than all reason." Thus, on the one hand, a social institution is measured by some social ideal, for example, justice in one or another of its various formulations. On the other hand, the whole social organization as such is questioned— and perhaps justified—by what lies beyond all social organizations, by what is "boundless," [by an infinite justice] as over against the actual life of justice. Again, the ethical maturity of any man is, on the one hand, measured by the ideal of ethical personality and his approximation to this ideal. On the other hand, the ethical personality as such in its maturity or immaturity is brought into question —and perhaps justified—by "the holy" that lies beyond all personality.

That which is beyond all form and criticizes the form as such, is not to be confused with the criticism whereby life brings spirit into question. Life itself is subject to criticism and that in two forms, one form emanating from the ideal and the other from beyond life. The criticism of life which emanates from the ideal measures life by criteria such as health, power, wealth, creativity. These ideals, however, are not themselves life, as the "philosophy of the vital"[3] believes them to be when it opposes life to spirit. For illness, weakness, poverty, and exhaustion are also to be found in life. It is spirit that lifts the ideal of life out of life's ambiguity, and occasionally—in what would seem to be a desire for self-destruction[4]— sets "life" over against itself. And just as "life" is not the locus from which rational criticism comes, so it is not the basis of prophetic criticism either. The fact that life itself questions and even destroys all forms of life is an element of life itself. Indeed, this cycle of creation and destruction is life. Prophetic criticism, however, raises the question whether or not this process of creation and negation is really the unity of life. Prophetic criticism does not favor negation over the creative process, nor does it favor creativity over negation.

---

[3] I use this term as a characterization of the most recent phase of *Lebens-philosophie* as represented by Klages and others.

[4] This "misology" (Hegel) of the spirit against itself today plays a considerable role among the younger generation.

It favors neither metaphysical pessimism that exalts death above life nor metaphysical optimism that affirms life against death. Prophetic criticism stands beyond all these possibilities, for it stands beyond life. And from "beyond life" it brings life into question.

Both kinds of criticism have their source in the act whereby man rises above mere being as such—and also above the immediacy of life as it is defined in the philosophy of vitalism. Rational criticism, has its sources in the rise of spirit above being; prophetic criticism in the shattering of life and spirit by that which is beyond both of them. Thus, both modes of criticism presuppose a break with the immediacy of being. The significance of this break, however, is different in each type of criticism. In the first case, criticism remains within the sphere of being; what is immediately given is measured by true being, the "given" is measured by what is sought after and also demanded.

Criticism has its starting point in being and at the same time is directed against it. Its presupposition is the bifurcation of being into that which is in conformity with its essence and that which is estranged from its essence. In the second case, criticism implies a transcending of existential being, whether it is in conformity with its essence or in opposition to it. This transcending of being is "faith." It is, therefore, absolutely contradictory to speak of a "religion within."[5] Although such a religion does involve the act of transcending being, this act really remains within the sphere that should be transcended. Where this attitude is predominant, prophetic criticism is inevitably identified with rational criticism and the unconditioned transcendent is confused with the conditioned transcendence of the spirit. The possibility of such a confusion—the essential characteristic of a self-sufficient and autonomous culture—makes it necessary for us to ask: How far do both kinds of criticism follow the same path and where do they separate? The following consideration is decisive for the answer to this question: if the criticism that proceeds from what is beyond being and spirit is genuine criticism, that is, if it has the power of "dividing," then it must not proceed in such a way as to question being and spirit merely *in abstracto*. This sort of questioning would not lead to a real divi-

---

[5] "Within mere reason" (Kant) or "within humanity" (Natorp).

sion (crisis), it would only leave everything as it was or, rather, it would leave concrete criticism—that is, effective criticism—to the rational approach. Thus we have here, on the one side, radically negative judgments concerning being as such, while on the other we find an extreme indifference to the critical situation that obtains within the existential sphere. It is clear that the former attitude as a reaction against self-sufficient autonomy has had a real justification both historically and in principle. It is equally clear, however, that the relationship obtaining between the two kinds of criticism is not in this way adequately dealt with.

In our day we hear frequent reference to the "existential" character of prophetic criticism. Certainly, it is well that our attention should have been directed to the significance of prophetic criticism and especially that the character of "unconditioned concern" that attaches to all really religious proclamation, should have been emphasized. But the concreteness of prophetic criticism is not sufficiently expressed by this characterization alone. For the decisive point here is the way in which the term "existential" is interpreted. Prophetic criticism can become concrete only if the "existential" embraces the entire sphere of actual being and in such a way that there is a "division" within it. Therefore the prophetic criticism of the Old Testament, the criterion of all genuinely prophetic criticism, always includes a concrete rational criticism. If so-called dialectical theology has in our generation been considered in any way to have a prophetic character, we find the explanation for it here. The prophetic character of dialectical theology was possible only because that theology was based upon a striking and forceful proclamation of what is "beyond both being and spirit." Thus dialectical theology was able to subject theology as it is today—that is, spirit—to a criticism that was at the same time a concrete criticism and, from the point of view of the ideal of theology (theology as it ought to be), a rational criticism. The effectiveness of dialectical theology was limited because it overlooked the indissoluble relationship between the theological ideal and all other ideals, and therefore of theological criticism and all other rational criticism; thus it unintentionally relegated everything having to do with theology to a separate domain of prophetic criticism. The effect of this was to weaken to some extent the religious criticism that had been directed against other cultural spheres, for example, the criticism that had been advanced by "religious socialism," and therefore to strengthen the existing forms and powers of the secular life.

This abstractly prophetic criticism (abstract not with regard to theology, but with regard to the intellectual life in general, the sciences, society, art, etc.) has been in its effect conservative. Moreover, by virtue of an imminent dialectic that was now set into operation by the very isolation of theology, this abstract criticism exercised a conservative influence upon theology itself. For theology was now cut off from the rational criticism that is always offered by the other cultural spheres. The separation of the two types of criticism has, as this development shows, brought about a weakening of the critical attitude in general. To be sure, the two types of criticism are not identical, but they do depend upon each other.

The criticism that proceeds from beyond being and spirit becomes concrete in the criticism that spirit directs against existential being, a criticism that rises within the realm of being itself. Prophetic criticism becomes concrete in rational[6] criticism. On the other hand, rational criticism acquires from prophetic criticism the quality of inevitability and unconditionedness. These several qualities give to prophetic criticism its existential character. Prophetic criticism raises the question of existence, and in an ultimate, unconditional way. Rational criticism cannot do this, for it cannot question being as such; it can only strive to bring about an approximation of "resistant" existence to true being. But this attempt does not possess the quality of inevitability, since being as such is not questioned. This means that all autonomous criticism receives its ultimate seriousness from the prophetic criticism standing behind it. A glance at history, for example, the history of social criticism, confirms this statement with overwhelming force.[7] But the other side of this is that the very process whereby rational criticism has been given its

6 In this whole discussion the word "rational" means: anything confined to or belonging intrinsically within the sphere of reason, anything connected with the formation of concepts and "ideal" constructions. An "ideal" can, however, be acquired in a very irrational way, for example, intuitively.

7 The dependence of the social criticism of the West upon the social criticism found in Old Testament prophetism and in the Christian sects has been sufficiently established.

own depth by prophetic criticism, reveals also the limitations inherent within it. The element in prophetic criticism on the basis of which being becomes problematic does not point to a fulfillment in the existential order. It, rather, provides fulfillment in a sphere that stands beyond the critical situation. This is expressed in the word "grace." Through grace even the criticism that has been given prophetic depth is in its turn subjected to criticism. Any ultimate right for it to negate and go beyond (*aufzuheben*) being is denied it. But this right is denied it only after it has itself advanced to the stage of unconditioned seriousness. Thus the question as to how far the two types of criticism follow the same path may now be answered. In rational criticism prophetic criticism becomes concrete. In prophetic criticism rational criticism finds both its depth and its limit: its depth through the unconditionedness of the demand, and its limit through grace.

b. Protestant Criticism

Protestant criticism is prophetic criticism. It possesses all the marks of prophetic criticism which have been characterized in the foregoing discussion; it proceeds from what is beyond being and spirit, and from this vantage point it renders both problematic. It is closely associated with rational criticism and gives to it its unconditioned seriousness. And as the herald of grace, it imposes its limits upon rational criticism.

This becomes clear in the whole conflict over justification, the critical concept peculiar to Protestantism. Justification proceeds from what is beyond being and spirit. It questions existence as such and it refuses to take any account of the fact that "resistant" existence may achieve a partial approximation to true being. Luther's struggle against the claim of reason to be able to grasp and realize truth on its own account expresses his conviction that truth transcends both being and spirit. And his struggle against the claims of free will in connection with justification expresses his conviction that justification transcends both spirit and freedom. It is absolutely erroneous to interpret Luther's struggle against reason as a fight against autonomy, and as perhaps a defense of heteronomy. His struggle, like that of all prophetic proclamation, was, rather, a denial of the self-sufficiency of autonomy; or, it was a protest against the confusion of spirit with what is beyond being and spirit. It is equally wrong to interpret Luther's struggle against free will as a denial of indeterminism and as perhaps a defense of determinism. His struggle, like that of all prophetic criticism, was a struggle against the confusion of freedom with what is beyond being and freedom. The zeal with which Luther carried on this whole struggle matches the danger that prophetic criticism, so effective in Luther's protest, may be dissolved into rational criticsm.

This danger was the greater, because Protestantism, in accord with the nature of prophetic criticism, not only appropriated the rational criticism of the church and civilization but also developed and intensified it. The "going back to the sources" that united Protestantism and humanism, arose, indeed, out of the desire to measure the actual situation in the church and civilization against the ideal. Scripture and antiquity were viewed not only as the sources from which Western culture originated but also as their ideal. Protestant criticism of Scholastic theology is, among other things, always criticism from the point of view of the classical biblical ideal of theological method. Protestant criticism of the church was, among other things, always criticism deriving from the biblical ideal of the medieval sects. Protestant criticism of Roman abuses was always at least partially criticism motivated by nationalistic feelings. And this has been all the more significant, because the Renaissance in no way considered itself to be a self-sufficient, autonomous culture. Rather, it viewed itself first of all˘and quite self-consciously as a religious regeneration of Christian society. There is little doubt that Luther's far-reaching historical influence was at least partly due to the fact that his thought had an integral relationship to all the significant forms of rational criticism of his age. And there is ample reason to fear that recent Protestant theology, since it has more and more destroyed this integral relationship, has missed the historical opportunity offered to it and also to contemporary Protestantism.[8] The picture of Luther which comes from this neo-Protestant group depicts him as entirely cut off from every relationship whatsoever to

[8] This is the more to be deplored since in its origin and in its first effects this more recent Protestant theology belonged to a concretely critical movement, that is, to religious socialism.

the rational criticism of the historical forces of his time.[9] The conception of Luther set forth by Holl and his school is by far superior to their picture.[10] But, like the neo-Protestant group, they also fail to take advantage of their opportunity to influence our period. Their message is rendered quite ineffective by the fact that they apply directly and immediately to the present those forms of rational criticism contained in Luther's prophetic word which are historically conditioned, instead of allowing them to burst forth anew out of the depths of the present, out of the Kairos.[11] At all events, it cannot be denied that in the original message of Protestantism prophetic criticism was combined with a broad rational criticism in such a way that rational criticism found there both its depth and its limit.

The third and decisive element in Luther's struggle and in his indictment of the church is his demand that criticism be overcome by grace. The phrases "imputation of righteousness to the sinner," "righteousness through faith alone," indicate what it is that overcomes the critical situation in its unconditioned depth. The Catholic doctrine of grace had made rational criticism a part of the idea of grace. According to this conception, grace is at least partially conditioned by the rise of freedom above being, by the approximation of "resistant" existence to true being. But this was possible only when at the same time the unconditioned seriousness of criticism was weakened. Indeed, this was consciously and deliberately accomplished in nominalistic theology. The struggle for "faith without works" is not the struggle of merely one way of salvation over against another; rather, it is the struggle for both unconditioned seriousness and the unconditioned conquest of criticism. In the first prophetic breakthrough of the Reformation this fact was understood almost without exception; later, after the disputed positions had been won, the meaning of the original breakthrough was lost in the consolidation and fortification of these positions. The period

[9] Cf. the attitude of Gogarten toward Luther, in particular in his epilogue to *De servo arbitrio.*

[10] Holl himself has frequently dealt with the rational criticism to be found in Luther's work.

[11] This explains why with few exceptions the interpretations of Luther offered today present him in an unfavorable light as far as they relate him to our general contemporary situation.

following the Reformation was in both Lutheranism and Calvinism devoted to unfortunate disputes over justification and predestination. These controversies led to a misinterpretation of these doctrines through the hypostatization of the transcendence of grace. But these doctrines are properly understood only if they are interpreted as pointing to the situation in which prophetic criticism is both fulfilled and overcome. Both concepts are correctives against the weakening of criticism and grace. And both concepts take on a fateful meaning as soon as they are supposed to represent processes that may be described by theology in an objectively metaphysical or religiously methodological sense. The discussions about double predestination—whether it is an actual event, or whether good works are an advantage or disadvantage for salvation—imply that genuine prophetic criticism has lost its power.[12]

Protestant criticism is prophetic criticism; it is prophetic criticism in the full sense in that it contains rational criticism which it drives to its depth and to its limit. From the beginning the burden of Protestantism is in this criticism. Criticism has always outweighed creation. Yet Protestantism does not lack the creative and formative principle; it cannot lack this principle any more than can any other reality. For form is the *prius* of crisis. Rational form is the presupposition of rational criticism; the form of grace is the presupposition of prophetic criticism.

2. PROTESTANTISM AS A CREATIVE AND FORMATIVE PRINCIPLE

a. The Two Kinds of Form-Creation

The presupposition of all rational criticism is rational creation of form. Criticism proceeds from the ideal. But one can discern the ideal only from the vantage point of a concrete form. The substance of every ideal is concrete; it reflects the concrete creation which the subject sees around him. Only the formal element of the ideal,

---

12 Such questions presuppose an objectified concept of God, a concept that permits one to make assertions about God as a metaphysical object. Such assertions differ—and to their disadvantage—from the old myth only in the fact that they interpret this metaphysical object in a rational, objective way. The protest against such a concept of God is one of the most pressing tasks of Protestant criticism.

the element that determines its character as an ideal, is abstract. This formal element is valid for all ideals and it is independent of any particular form. And yet, the abstract, formal element of the ideal can be grasped as such only because it is itself conditioned by a particular form, namely, by that form in which the form shows a tendency toward its own dissolution—a dissolution into abstraction. This peculiar and rare phenomenon, however, should not be made into a norm. The apprehension of the abstract character of the ideal without any underlying form, as, for example, with Kant, presupposes an intellectual and social form the essence of which is the dissolution of the form.[13] It is by no means necessary, however, that the process of dissolution should have advanced very far; it is only necessary that such a tendency be actually present and characterize the form. If this is the case, the very awareness of the tendency toward dissolution may itself hasten the dissolution. At all events, the Kantian form of rational criticism represents a special case. And it is absolutely inappropriate to establish any especially intimate relation between this form of criticism and the prophetic criticism characteristic of Protestantism. On the contrary, there is really no more impotent form of criticism than Kantian criticism. For it is not upheld by the power of an emerging form. It is abstract and condemned to be merely a subject for academic debate; at the most it can only obstruct concrete criticism. When Protestantism combined with Kantian criticism, it allied itself with theory against practice, with a formless society against the emerging social forms, with the impotence of abstraction against the power of concrete intuition. Kantianism *(Kritizismus)* is criticism; but its ideal is the ideal of an abstract society which dissolves all concrete forms [into abstraction]. It is an abstract ideal in which all particular contents based upon import are destroyed and nothing but the merely formal element of the ideal survives. If "dialectical theology" really intends to unite once again with Kantian criticism[14] (the previous union between theology and Kantianism brought about

---

13 It is a characteristic feature of the bourgeois form of society that in it from the outset the tendency toward dissolution of the form is predominant.

14 Cf. Brunner among others. To me this seems to be symbolic of the fact that Protestantism is once again withdrawing from the sphere of the concrete decisions of the Kairos and thus in actuality making its decision for the status quo.

by Ritschl adopted many essentially humanistic elements from Kant, the apostle of Enlightenment), it reveals by that very fact its indifference to genuine rational criticism. It chooses Kant as the creator of criticism, because he does not embarrass it by forcing it to make a real decision within the rational, critical sphere. For if everything is criticized, then in principle nothing is criticized; and what already is enjoys an advantage that remains unquestioned. Thus dialectical theology overlooks the fact that it has in actuality made a concealed decision in favor of middle-class society, a society that is moving toward the dissolution of all forms [into abstraction] and a society in which only abstract criticism is possible. This discussion shows that all rational criticism proceeds from a given form and that even Kantian criticism still has its roots in a form that in actuality destroys all form. But the relationship between ideal and form should not be interpreted as if the ideal were merely an image of the actual existing form. For in that case the ideal would not be able to go beyond the form, it would not be able to subject the form to criticism. The ideal is, rather, the expression of an emerging form that arises out of the tensions existing within an actual form. Form in the spiritual and social sense is always (among other things) emerging form. The most stable social institutions have within them a tendency to develop under the attraction of the ideal which is always a step beyond them. Consequently, we are not here concerned with the problem posed by the fact that reality is always in a state of approximation to the ideal. The ideal of any society is never realized merely by the average members of society or through their attitudes but, rather, through those institutions, activities, and personalities that have a symbolic character. Once these latter forms have acquired a symbolic power, the ideal is really fulfilled. For all fulfillment is representative. This is the logical relationship that obtains between ideal and fulfillment. It is certainly no merely mechanical coming together of the real and the ideal. No significant meaning can be associated with such a mechanical juxtaposition. One reason for this is that the ideal is never to be seen in a visible form but is always represented only by symbols.

Rational criticism is the criticism directed by the emerging form to the form that is passing away. This is the source of its concreteness and its power. But it would seem to be also the source of its accidental and indifferent value. For the mere succession of forms one after the other is not a process that one can observe or participate in as if it merited unconditioned seriousness. Rational criticism would lose its intrinsic zeal if it spoke only in the name of the emerging form. In actuality this description of rational criticism is entirely inadequate. Rational criticism contains within itself the abstract element inherent in the ideal as such. And this element is effective whenever anything is measured by a concrete ideal. It is true, however, that it is not effective in any visible or tangible way. It is the error of Kantianism that it believes that it can in a clear and definite way isolate the abstract element of the ideal, the element that makes the ideal an ideal, and that it can then make use of this abstract element for the purposes of actual criticism. It is just this, however, that is responsible for the impotence of Kantian criticism. Indeed, Kantianism is nothing less than an expression of the very principle of dissolution. In really concrete criticism, that is, in really powerful criticism, the abstract element of the ideal is enveloped within the concrete element; this abstract element is the most profound element in concrete criticism and gives to it its unconditioned seriousness. But it cannot in itself be grasped intellectually. The seriousness of rational criticism depends upon that which makes the ideal an ideal, that is, upon its quality of being ideal. But it is impossible to analyze this quality by abstraction and then to use it to measure reality. There is no such thing as a general abstract ideal of the state, of marriage, of architecture, or of methodology. But within any ideal that is critically invoked there lies the ideal as such, as implicit seriousness. Although this ideal element can be abstractly formulated it cannot in its abstractness be given any immediate practical application.[15]

In any truly living ideal the universal quality of ideal being is embedded in a concreteness that reaches down to the realm of life.

---

[15] A genuine ideal is the intuitive perception of an emerging form, of a *Gestalt* that is coming into being. The ideal is realized on the coming into existence of the new form. We determine whether a new form has come into existence by examining the basic structural elements. (Once a change in these elements has taken place, the other less fundamental aspects of the *Gestalt* begin gradually to be affected.) Only through them are individual processes gradually defined.

The living substance of every entity has a different quality. The most primitive reactions to the external world, even sense impressions, are together determined by the general character of this vital structure as a whole. The same thing holds for man's reactions to concrete psychic and social realities which likewise stand in a mutual relationship with his vital structure or *Gestalt*. These realities are involved in every ideal and consequently in all rational criticism. The tendencies of the living, psychic, social substance include an ideal quality. Through these tendencies the ideal receives its power, and criticism its creative force. This justifies all those attempts to interpret spirit in terms of life and to interpret the formation of an ideal from social and psychic existence.[16] It must be admitted, however, that the philosophical elaboration of these tendencies was greatly hindered by their futile opposition to Kantianism. These ideas entered into the general consciousness in a popularized form that could easily be refuted philosophically; and yet they have had a strong and frequently disastrous influence that has been both critical and hostile to criticism.[17] Only when these tendencies are united with a purified critical consciousness can they lead to an adequate theory of the way in which ideals come into existence as well as to a theory of rational criticism and of rational form-creation.

The ideal element, the quality that makes an ideal what it is, and which operates in a hidden way in the formation of ideals, gives to the ideal its seriousness. It also gives to prophetic criticism its possibility of uniting with rational criticism as well as its possibility of appropriating the concrete ideal. But this presupposes that prophetic criticism is itself supported by some being, by some religious form from which criticism proceeds. But here there arises the difficulty that this being which is the basis of prophetic criticism is "something beyond being and freedom." This cannot be concretely grasped, however, as one can grasp a living form. Nor

16 This has been done to the highest degree in the social sphere by Marx and in the psychological sphere by Nietzsche and depth-psychology. It is not an accident that only because of this the philosophy of the nineteenth century became a creative factor in history.

17 We have in mind here the fanaticism with which orthodox Marxists frequently use the concept of ideology to upset opposing intellectual attitudes.

does it belong to the sphere of becoming but, rather, it bears in every relationship the character of the "beyond" as such. Nor should it be identified with the religious forms and the changes to which they they are subject. Religious forms as such belong entirely to the rational sphere; and everything said here about the becoming of form, about the critical ideal and its twofold character, holds for them also. Religious reality, like other realities, extends, on the one side, right into the biological realm[18] and, on the other side, it conceals within itself a universal and ideal character. Every religion, every religious formulation of an ideal, indeed all religious criticism can be understood in the light of this idea. But this does not provide any understanding of the real import of religion. The ultimate point of reference of religion is beyond the sphere of realization, it completely transcends the whole interplay and opposition between being and spirit.

If prophetic criticism speaks in the name of any being at all, this being must be a transcendent being, which, despite its transcendent character, must also belong to reality. But the transcendent reality as something present is what we may call grace. Prophetic criticism must burst forth from the reality of grace or—to keep the analogy— it must issue from a form of grace.[19] The form of grace—in this phrase the whole problem of religious form-creation is implied. In defining the concept which is supposed to be expressed in these words we must take care to avoid especially two false interpretations that would lead us astray. One of these misinterprets the bond between prophetic and rational criticism as identity. Consequently it supposes that the *Gestalt* of grace is to be found in the rational form that has reached its highest perfection. It confuses intuiting the ideal and being grasped by grace. Grace is drawn into the tension between being and spirit. Therefore, it is no longer able by its appearance to overcome this tension. Thus the vantage point of prophetic criticism is surrendered. The other error comes

18 The psychology of religion from the beginning (Xenophanes) has emphasized this relationship in the clearest way.
19 I select this term, although it is subject to all sorts of misunderstandings, in order to give the clearest possible expression to the analogy with the rational form. The meaning of this term is to be understood only in connection with the discussion that follows.

from inferring that grace is something objective because it is present. Grace becomes fixed and tangible; it is conceived as a higher note of reality but as tangible in the same way as any other reality. The form of grace becomes an existential form of a higher order; it is, for example, identified with a church to which the administration of the substance of grace is entrusted.[20] Thus the prophetic criticism of any existential reality is rendered impossible. In the name of the *"Gestalt* of grace," one form of being is made exempt from criticism. But if prophetic criticism is thus restricted within certain limits the unconditionedness of grace is vitiated and broken. For now a special intellectual attitude is required in order to make the fixated form of grace effective. In order to bring grace under control, certain laws are now set up which are themselves not grace, as for instance the *jus divinum* of Catholicism or the demand of Protestant orthodoxy that any doubts concerning the Scriptures or the "pure doctrine" should be suppressed as blasphemous and culpable.

The form of grace is neither a rational or ideal form nor an existential form of a higher order. In both cases the essential quality of grace is destroyed because of preoccupation with the form. As a result one might infer that it is necessary to give up the whole conception, the form of grace. Indeed, this is just what dialectical theology has demanded. Yet it is content with only making the demand. But even dialectical theology is nevertheless compelled to indicate the being from whom its prophetic criticism proceeds (or, to put it in the language of dialectical theology: from whom the theological formulation of prophetic criticism proceeds). But if it does designate the basis of its criticism and speaks, for example, of the "Holy Spirit," the idea of the "form of grace" is necessarily included. This idea is unavoidable, for it is the presupposition of any criticism uttered with ultimate power and authority (as the word of God).

The form of grace is the form of that which lies beyond being and freedom, as far as it appears in the tension between being and freedom. And yet it exists; and as something existing it can be intuitively perceived. But if it exists as a manifestation of what transcends being, and as such it is incomprehensible, it cannot be

---

[20] This is a strictly literal definition of the concept of "supernaturalism."

"fixed," it cannot be made an object. Grace is something present but not something objective. It is actual in objects, not as an object but as the transcendent meaning of an object. The form of grace is a form of [transcendent] meaning. The *Gestalt* of any holy person is, on the one hand, a form of being, including all that belongs to his spiritual and physical existence even if he has reached the stage of ideal perfection. On the other hand, he symbolizes something that cannot be objectively demonstrated to be in him, something that transcends being and spirit and yet something that determines the special meaning, the real significance, of his *Gestalt*. Thus reality can become the bearer of a meaning that unconditionally transcends it. And wherever this meaning exists, we have a form or *Gestalt* of grace. This is the ultimate possibility that supports and gives meaning to being; and where this possibility is realized it can be intuitively perceived. The holy is not imperceptible. But it is no object. The holy is perceived as something that is not objective; it is perceived as a transcendent meaning. The controversy between Catholicism and Protestantism on the visibility or invisibility of the church is to be decided in the light of these considerations. The church as a form of grace can be intuitively perceived, but it is not an objective reality. In the church that which transcends being and freedom can be perceived as the transcendent meaning of the church but not as its empirical, supernatural quality. An "invisible" church would not be a form of grace. It would not have the power of prophetic criticism. Only in so far as it is a *Gestalt* of grace can the church proclaim the crisis with absolute power and authority. Thus we may summarize: the visible church is essentially a form of grace, but this does not mean that it has a tangible, objective form. The church does not have the form of grace at its disposal. The form of grace cannot be the basis of any "system" or of any hierarchical pretense. The church has the form of grace by meaning or signifying something. To mean something involves more than merely pointing to it. Anything that merely points to something else may remain external to it. But anything that means or signifies something is formed by the reality of that which it signifies. The *Gestalt* of grace involves more than merely pointing to the transcendent. It is the "Glory of God" becoming visible. The protest against the hierarchical objectification of the form of grace in the form of the church should not be interpreted as ruling out every possibility of perceiving the "Glory" of the church.[21]

The relationship between the perceptibility and the nonobjective character of the form of grace may be defined as "anticipation." Inherent in anticipation is a temporal image of a perfect consummation that is coming. This temporal image is a symbolic form essential to all eschatological thinking; it cannot be dispensed with, although its directness can be broken. But if it is used—even as something "broken"—then the form of grace may be characterized as an anticipation of what is beyond both freedom and being. In this sense all mysticism is anticipation, provided of course that it is not a technique of anticipation. For as technique mysticism is merely an aspect of the tension between freedom and being.[22] In this sense also, visions are anticipations, provided of course one does not "glory" in them, that is, provided one does not regard them as objects of possession.[23] Thus the sacramental death and resurrection, the descent of the spirit, the "knowledge of God," and "love" as a quality of the "new creature" are anticipations; they are modes of participation in the form of grace, but they should never be received as "possessions."[24] For the concept of anticipation implies that the thing anticipated *cannot yet* be appropriated, that anticipation is at it were a figurative laying hold of something that is imbued with meaning, but which must not be objectified.

We must now ask how the form of grace is related to the rational forms. The answer to this question may be stated in principle in this way: the form of grace is realized only in rational forms and in such a way that, on the one hand, it gives to them a meaning that transcends them, while, on the other hand, it unites with the particular meaning inherent in the rational forms. Thus we find here the same relationship as that existing between prophetic and

[21] For similar attempts to clarify the idea of "a *Gestalt* of the church," see the *Berneuchener Buch* published by the Berneuchener Conference (Hamburg, 1926), and also *Das Alter der Kirche*, edited by Rosenstock and Wittig.

[22] The controversy over mysticism can be settled in principle if we distinguish between mysticism as a technique and mysticism as a form of grace.

[23] Cf. II Cor. 12.

[24] On this point I agree with Barth's eschatological interpretation of I Cor. 13. But Barth overlooks the fact that the discussion of eschatological fulfillment is possible only by "anticipation" through the form of grace.

rational criticism. Prophetic criticism transcends rational criticism and yet at the same time incorporates it within itself. "Love is the fulfillment of the law," "Spirit guideth into all truth," that is, the form of grace is a fulfillment of the rational form, not in an empirically conceivable way but in an anticipatory sense pregnant with meaning. It is not on its own level that righteousness is improved or increased by love, nor knowledge by truth. Rather, they receive a *new dimension*, a dimension that is to be seen in the existential order and which reveals its transcendent meaning. The form of grace includes within itself the forms of righteousness and of knowledge. But it does not stand in the tension obtaining between being and spirit, the level on which these forms have their existence. It stands beyond this tension and reveals—by way of anticipation—a transcendent righteousness that has not been won in the face of opposition and that has not been wrested from something that resists it.

The different expressions of the form of grace belong to what one may call "religious culture." They are subject to criticism, to rational as well as to prophetic criticism. Indeed, they are the special object of prophetic criticism. For it is the continual task of prophetic criticism to fight against the confusion of the "form of grace" with "religious culture." It is the objectification of the form of grace that leads to this confusion. Here, it is manifest in man's attempt to exploit grace in order to escape criticism. On the other hand, the relationship that obtains between the form of grace and religious culture really justifies religious culture. Religious culture is the epitome of all those forms in which the rational form expresses its transcendent meaning and in which the rational form receives by anticipation the character of a form of grace. The existential forms of all churches and of all individual piety have this meaning. They are nothing in themselves. In themselves, they are merely rational forms; but they express a transcendent meaning that can appear in the rational forms.

There is a danger that these forms of expression may claim to be the immediate expression of the form of grace. But the form of grace is not bound to them; it can appear also in rational forms that produce no explicit forms of religious expression. The holy can appear in the garment of secularism, although this garment is a disguise. The possibility represents by its mere existence a criticism of the claim of any religious culture to be itself a form of grace. This is the burden and the threat of secularism for the religious man. It shows him the limits of religious culture, it proves that grace can operate independently of religious culture. Yet this does not give priority to secular culture; for it too is in danger of denying the form of grace in favor of a mere self-enclosed form of being, and of becoming autonomous, cutting itself off from any transcendent meaning. The relationship between being and what is beyond being carries with it the implication that a form of being that in principle denies the form of grace is thereby threatened with the loss of its own form. Just as prophetic criticism gives to rational criticism its unconditioned, and thus its transcendent, significance, so grace gives to every rational form the power to be, that is, the power to participate in unconditioned or transcendent being. Anything that stood *only* under the threat, *only* in the tension between being and freedom would be absolutely impotent. Only by virtue of the hidden presence of a supporting element coming from beyond freedom and being can living form participate in being. There is, therefore, in every living form a hidden form of grace that is identical with its power to be. Of course, the living form does not thereby become a form of grace. For it remains in the opposition that obtains between being and freedom. The form of grace appears only where this conflict is overcome. And this is the very goal toward which the life of all forms is directed; this is the meaning implicit in every form, a meaning that can be fulfilled but that can also be missed. An autonomy that relies upon itself leads to the loss of form, because it misses the form of grace and thus surrenders in principle the power to be. The tendency toward the dissolution of form, which is the basis for understanding the abstract principle of rational criticism, may consequently be interpreted as a missing or squandering of grace. The alliance of Protestantism with this abstract principle of rational criticism will thus be seen to be a union with a principle that lacks both grace and the power of being. In reality this form of being (rational criticism), like many another, lives on the inheritance of the form of grace out of which it was born, namely, the Protestant Christian tradition.

One question has so far not been answered, namely, the question

as to how a change in the form of grace can take place, that is, how
what is beyond being and freedom can appear in different forms of
being. The answer can be derived by a consideration of the relationship between criticism and form. The realization of grace is related
in a special way to prophetic criticism. To the extent and in the
way in which prophetic criticism determines the character of a
form of being, grace can be realized in it. Of course, there is no
question here of temporal succession. The assertion that the *prius*
of criticism is the form also holds true here. But the understanding
of a form of grace is possible only if we consider the relationship
that obtains in it between grace and criticism. Finally, there is
always the question as to how far grace is used (or rather abused)
in order to escape radical prophetic criticism; or, to express the
same idea in another way, we must ask how far the form of grace
has been demonized. The antidemonic struggle of prophetic criticism is decisive for the form of grace; it determines the way in
which what is beyond being and freedom appears within being.
Only on this basis is it possible to understand the changes that the
forms of grace undergo and thus to understand indirectly the
changes that take place in the historical forms in general, in those
forms that have been shaped by history.[25] It is also from this point
of view that we may understand the characteristic element of the
Protestant principle.

b. The Creative and Formative Powers of Protestantism

Grace is the *prius* of criticism. But every form in which grace appears must itself be subjected to criticism. This means that grace
must not be objectified. This description is itself derived from the
basic Protestant attitude. So far as *historical* Protestantism is concerned, however, the idea of grace has been applied mainly in a
negative way, that is, in the rejection of the Catholic objectification
of grace and of the autonomous secularization of it. The positive
approach to be set forth here represents an attempt to analyze the
problem in a new way and to solve it both according to the Protestant principle and on the basis of the present situation. For the
positive solution traditionally offered by Protestantism has broken

25 Cf. the chapter on "The Demonic," in my book *The Interpretation of
History* (New York: Scribners, 1936).

down, and this has driven Protestantism itself to the verge of collapse.

There is one form of grace that Protestantism preserved after having shattered all other forms of grace, namely, Scripture. Scripture was viewed as a perfect union of prophetic criticism and of religious form. And by appealing to Scripture all sacramental objectification seemed to be rendered impossible. It is well known, and it has often been commented on, that in spite of this a new objectification arose within Protestantism. As a result of its literal interpretation of Scripture, the church has fixed the form of grace by reducing it to pure doctrine. The purely symbolic character of Scripture as an anticipation of the form of grace was not appreciated. Hence, there naturally arose the claim to possess the truth, a claim that was allegedly exempt from prophetic criticism and very early fell a victim to rational criticism.

A further problem arose from the fact that it is always necessary to give the form of grace contemporaneity. For grace is really grace only if it is present. This was a most difficult problem for Protestantism. Protestantism found itself in a situation very different from that of primitive Christianity. In late antiquity, religious forms were available through which a new form of grace could appear, and appear in the only way that is truly effective, namely, in and through the medium of prophetic criticism. Outstanding among these forms were the Jewish idea of the chosen people who had been given the Promise, and Hellenistic sacramentalism, which as a rule strove to overcome the old demonized forms of paganism. Already in the New Testament, Christianity combined its original message with these forms in order to create a new religious form, the form represented later by Catholicism. This union was, to be sure, effected in a well-nigh unconscious fashion and as though it were merely a foregone conclusion, though it was always under the stimulus and influence of radical prophetic criticism. Protestantism did not have at its disposal such a variety of "earthen vessels" for the reception of its message of grace. And the older forms had been demonized in the course of the evolution of the Catholic Church.[26] Thus Prot-

---

[26] Cf. the description of this development in my article "Rechtfertigung und Zweifel," Vorträge der Theologischen Konferenz zu Giessen, No. 39 (Giessen, 1924).

estantism would have remained within the sphere of pure protest, that is, it would have destroyed itself as a reality if the possibility for new forms had not arisen within Catholicism itself. Protestantism finds a connecting point with Catholicism by laicizing the monastic ideal of interior discipline. The monastic ideal located the form of grace in the center of the ethical personality while it abandoned the sacramental objectification of the holy. From this attitude arose Luther's protest against the entire system of the hierarchical objectification of grace as well as against the monkish, ascetic ideal as such. But there was no longer any holy form as such, and even if there were, it would now be found in that community of personalities where perfect love and truth prevail. Anything that claims to be sacred and that does not recognize the demand of the Unconditional is demonic. Here prophetic criticism identifies itself with ethical, rational criticism. But by this very fact the *Gestalt* of grace is deprived of its basis. The Catholic saint is holy apart from his personal ethical perfection. By virtue of the fact that he is the incarnation of the deepest meaning of life, he represents what is "beyond being and freedom." The Protestant, on the other hand, is holy not because he symbolizes a form of grace but, rather, because he has received the forgiveness of sins. He is holy in his unholiness. Here the application of the concept of holiness necessarily involves a paradox, and hence it can never result in a form or *Gestalt*. Grace is a judgment; it is not a visible reality. When prophetic criticism is identified with ethical, rational criticism, there can be no form of grace. But another form is engendered, a form of immeasurable historical significance, namely, the heroic personality. The heroic personality is aware of the boundary situation of man and always subjects himself to prophetic as well as to ethical rational criticism. His seriousness, his dignity, his great majesty—to use a term often applied to Calvin—is based on the fact that he refuses to allow the depths of prophetic criticism to be covered over and hidden by any objective form of grace. But this greatness is at the same time its danger. For it is almost inevitable that, in the absence of any form, the rational form of the ethical personality will take the decisive place and that rational criticism will engulf all prophetic criticism. This leads easily to a merging with the humanistic ideal of personality, and then the process of secularization is complete. This secularizing process goes through to its end because it is not obstructed by any holy form or *Gestalt*—a holy form in the sense in which we have used this term, a form that is visible though not objective. As a result even the heroic element is cut off from its roots and further development leads to a general breakdown of the *Gestalt* of personality, both as a reality and as an ideal.[27]

The necessary course of this development is always retarded by the fact that within Protestantism the *Gestalt* of grace has never disappeared completely. Since the form of grace is precisely the presupposition of prophetic criticism, it could never be really absent where prophetic criticism is effective. The Protestant is holy because of the judgment that is pronounced upon him, but this is true only if he applies this judgment to himself, that is, only if he has faith. But faith is possible only by virtue of the Holy Spirit, that is, in a form of grace. The implications of this conception have been recognized by "the theology of piety" from the pre-Pietism of the Reformation down to the fellowship-movements of our own time. Undoubtedly an indispensable element of every religious tradition has been preserved in this way, or at least some suggestion or hint of the form of grace has been kept alive. The history of Protestant piety shows how strong the influence of this residue has been, even though this influence has nearly always operated from outside the official church and in numerous ways analogous to Catholicism. The radical dissolution of this idea by Ritschl constitutes the reverse side of this tendency, since in Ritschl's thought prophetic criticism was absorbed by rational criticism and the form of grace was displaced by an ideal realm of moral personalities.

The decisive difference between the Pietist and the Catholic conceptions of holiness is that, in line with Protestant theory as a whole, the Pietist conception makes everything depend upon the subjective aspect of piety. Thus Pietism also fails to recognize that the holy possesses an objective reality in some sense or other. Piety remains in the tension that obtains between being and spirit. It does not proceed out of that which is beyond being and spirit. It therefore has within it a tendency toward secularism, a tendency to be absorbed

<hr />

[27] I have attempted to give a description of this breakdown, in "The Idea and the Ideal of Personality," in *The Protestant Era*. (Chicago: University of Chicago Press, 1948).

by a rational form. It is inclined to become an aesthetic sense of being in the world which prides itself on being above the sphere of moral struggle. Hence, even in the impetus that Protestantism has given to the development of individual personality it has had a creative influence of the greatest historical importance.[28] But the ultimate consequence has been to bring about an emptying of the self-sufficient and self-centered personality, an outcome that is very largely characteristic of an aesthetic sense of being in the world (*Weltgefühl*).

All this serves to provide us with a new point of view with regard to the creative powers of Protestantism. The significance of these powers is frequently underrated, because it is not as easy to understand them as it is those of Catholicism. The difficulty of understanding them may be explained by the fact that Protestantism does not recognize any tangible form of grace as does Catholicism. Therefore, Protestantism is always exposed to the danger of becoming secularized. And it is extremely difficult to distinguish within modern autonomous culture those particular elements decisively determined by Protestantism, from the other elements. And yet, it is possible to do so as soon as one recognizes that the shaping (*Gestaltung*) of the personal life, whether in the sense of developing the ethical personality or in that of deepening the inner religious experience, is the real creative principle of Protestantism. Thus we see that both the bourgeois personality and the romantic personality have a Protestant character. Protestantism could never have become an historical reality had it not shown such a formative and creative power. And Protestantism would never have been driven to the limits of its existence, if its forms had not fallen into dissolution from within. Yet in this fate the greatness and the heroism of its creative principle is revealed.

Though it is less significant, the power of the creative principle

---

[28] Schleiermacher symbolizes this tendency in a marked degree. Catholic romanticism is to be distinguished from Protestant romanticism by the fact that it has always attempted to bring about a restoration of the form of grace as a tangible reality, and consequently it has inevitably exercised an influence favoring the ecclesiastical hierarchy. Protestant romanticism, on the other hand, has had an effect on certain movements of subjective piety, in particular the Great Awakening, which in the end has proved quite barren from an ecclesiastical point of view.

of Protestantism can be seen more clearly in the specifically religious sphere, that is, in its whole process of positing the forms in which the form of grace may express itself directly. Protestantism did not originally create such forms, for it lacked the form of grace in behalf of which it would have been meaningful to create them. The self-restraint of Protestantism in this respect constitutes its greatness. The fact that complete restraint was not and could not be maintained is to be explained by the general rule that form is always the *prius* of criticism. Thus Protestantism selected from the wealth of material in Catholicism what was suited for the purpose of transmitting prophetic criticism and the scriptural message of grace to the individual. This explains the origin of the congregation, which is supposed to pass on to the individual the "pure doctrine" found in Scripture; hence, the proper function of the parish is to provide the sermon and the catechetical, liturgical preparation and guidance for understanding the sermon. But the congregation is rarely if ever thought of as a visible form of grace. Hence, Protestantism is deprived of any real power in this religious sphere of creative cultural activity. (Yet even this reduced or "broken" creative power in Protestantism, viewed merely as an indication of its continuing opposition to Catholicism's objectification of grace, has had an immense historical significance.) From this point of view the decline in its power of attraction is quite understandable. It is possible at any time for the individual immediately to confront Scripture and apply it to himself without any reference to the church's official interpretation of it. And this holds true unconditionally as soon as it is believed that the content of Scripture can be understood only from an autonomous point of view. As a result, the leaders of autonomous culture, the creative representatives of the intellectual life, take the place of those who preach in the church. But even those who still feel the need of abiding by and submitting to the objective norm of Scripture expect nevertheless to receive a decisive stimulus from the preacher's subjective reflections; hence, they destroy the objective significance of listening to the Word. It would be futile and mistaken to attempt to rebuild the Protestant church by means that properly belong to the sphere of rational form-creation, whether such means be aesthetic or social in character. Either the Protestant church is a form of grace and then it has its meaning in itself; or it is not a form of grace and then it is impossible for it to gain new strength as a church by appropriating some meaning that is alien to it.

In this alternative we have come upon the most pressing question to be considered. Can Protestantism become in reality a form of grace and at the same time maintain its unswerving pursuit of prophetic criticism, a criticism that it cannot weaken without destroying its own character? The basic answer to this question has already been given in our exposition of the uniquely Protestant conception of the *Gestalt* of grace. And from this, other implications may be derived which apply to all aspects of theology, in particular to systematic and practical theology. We can touch only briefly on a few points here. We have said that the form of grace, as understood in the spirit of Protestantism, is not an objective form that can be "fixed." This has two fundamental implications. First, the relationship between the form of grace and the secular forms cannot be determined by setting up any merely objective lines of demarcation. The form of grace cuts across the secular realm. The forms of religious culture in which the form of grace lives are forms in which secularism assumes a transcendent significance, forms that anticipate what is beyond being and freedom. These forms of religious culture, therefore, remain in strict correlation with secularism. They do not constitute a special domain, a religious sphere that may be objectively delimited; they create no *sanctum* or *sanctissimum* in contrast to the *profanum*. The dissolution of the antithesis of the sacred and the profane represents the profoundest aspect of the Protestant principle. It is the first and the decisive consequence of the prophetic protest of Protestantism against the objectification of grace. This is the greatness of the Protestant principle, and as has been shown, it is also the danger by which it is threatened. The dissolution of the sphere of the holy as a special domain is by no means to be construed as a romantic consecration of a self-enclosed and self-sufficient autonomous culture. The protest against any special domain of the holy is implicit in every religious attitude; and the protest cannot be expressed except by establishing special forms above and beside culture. The form of grace may be veiled, but still it must shine through.

On the other hand, these forms must show that their "above" and "beside" are to be understood only as "above" and "beside" in the sense of meaning, of anticipation, and not as something above and beside objective being. Religious affirmations, for example, should not claim to be assertions concerning a higher objective order. They are, rather, affirmations in which the transcendent significance of all objects finds its special expression. The congregation should not consider itself to be a higher sociological form above the other forms of social life but, rather, an explicit expression of the transcendent significance of all sociological forms. But in order for it to be an explicit expression, specific media and special sociological groups must be created. This cannot be avoided if the form of grace is really to achieve form. But what is decisive here is that these special forms do not pretend to be in themselves something peculiar and different from the secular forms of existence; they purport, rather, to be only the bearers of the transcendent significance of these secular forms. What has to be avoided here is the dissolution of the church into the structures of society and the dissolution of religious knowledge into secular knowledge. What is required is the sort of church in which the social forms may contemplate the representation of their own transcendent import of meaning and the anticipation of their own ultimate goal beyond being and freedom. And with regard to knowledge, what is required is that sort of religious knowledge in which the secular cognitive attitude can by anticipation perceive the transcendental meaning of its own struggle for truth. In short, there appears in the church a new dimension of life, the dimension of its transcendence.

Yet we have in the church a form in the same dimension as all other forms; hence, it cannot properly make any unconditional claim. The power of the church is that power by which the forms of life are driven forward to the knowledge and the realization of their transcendent meaning. This is accomplished by a prophetic criticism that includes within it a rational criticism; and it is accomplished by means of an anticipation of the realization of all those intellectual and social forms, in which their transcendent significance is revealed. But neither through its criticism nor through its creative activity should the church when confronting the intellectual and social powers descend to the level on which these powers exist. The church is not a party, not even when in its prophetic criticism it adopts the claims of a party and reveals the transcendent significance of those claims, not even when in its anticipatory creative activity it approaches a rational form. The process whereby the church becomes concrete, the process whereby it assumes form, is never an unambiguous decision for a concrete form of being. Rather, even when a decision is involved, it is a decision that approves not a form of being in itself, but the transcendent meaning inherent in it.[29]

The second basic consequence resulting from the objectification of the form of grace is to be seen in its relationship to emerging forms, in short, to history. A form of grace that has been objectively fixated raises the forms in which it appears—the rational forms that it absorbs into itself—above the level of change. As does the Catholic Church, it must identify a specific rational ideal, for example, Thomism, with the form of grace. To be able to do so the church must conceive of the realm of ideas as static, as a system of essences which can be grasped once and for all; and once an understanding of this system has been achieved, it is assumed that it can never be surpassed. Consequently, on this basis, history has no decisive significance. The possibility of there being something essentially new is in principle denied to history. For essential reality is extrahistorical and supratemporal. On the other hand, from the point of view of a Protestantism that opposes any tendency to objectify grace, the realm of essences is dynamic. Something new is posited within the realm of essences. History is the *locus* of the essences. The idea exists within history, not beyond it. The form of grace always strives for realization in the changing historical forms. It must follow the way that leads between the pole of static self-possession, on the one hand, and complete self-abandonment, on the other. The form of grace is a living, struggling form. And yet, in every moment of its realization one can perceive something that stands beyond the struggle. The anticipation, the transcendent meaning, remains unchanged. But the rational form, in which the *Gestalt* of grace ap-

---

[29] This is the reason for the much criticized ambiguity of religious socialism, as it was represented, for example, by the *Blätter für religiösen Sozialismus.* This ambiguity, however, is expressed even in the name "religious socialism." And it is understandable only on the basis of the relationship obtaining between the form of grace and the emergence of concrete forms. From this point of view, however, the ambiguity is necessary and corresponds to the ambiguity inherent in all realization as over against what is beyond being and freedom.

pears, does change. Both the *Gestalt* of grace as a living form and history as the *locus* of the realization of essence are included within the Protestant principle and must be derived from it. The idea of Kairos as fulfilled time or as the realization of the form of grace in a new entity is a concept that attempts to make clear this aspect of the Protestant principle.[30]

When the idea of a form of grace is adopted by Protestantism and somehow brought to reality, then Protestant personalism is by that very fact overcome; and this holds for the psychological as well as for the social aspect of Protestant personalism. Grace as a perceptible reality cannot be thought of as operating directly at the center of personality, that is, as operating at the moment of decision. It is to be seen only in what has already been decided. It operates on the psychic and social level that upholds the personality and makes specific decisions possible. What is already decided and fulfilled, the anticipation of the eschaton in the existential order, is the locus at which the form of grace appears. From this it follows that the directing and shaping of the social, of the psychic, and even of the biological levels of existence is a pressing concern for Protestant form-creation. But this must be done in such a way and only in such a way that the center of the personality nevertheless remains a focal point in the religious relationship, the relationship to the Unconditional. For only at the center of the personality can that radical prophetic criticism be heard which sweeps aside all securities of a psychic and social character. It is necessary, however, that the isolation of the heroic personality and of the devout personality from their own psychic depths and from the supporting fabric of society be broken down. Just as form is the *prius* of criticism, so is the psychic and social form the *prius* of personal decision. Religious socialism, which should be and already has been in part supplemented by a religious depth–psychology, has attempted to deal with the situation in these terms and thus to prepare the way for a Protestant form of grace. The outcome of the revolutionary changes that are necessary here and that are already under way, cannot be predicted in our present situation.

If now the question be asked why the Protestant principle should

[30] Cf. My detailed discussion of this in the chapter on "Kairos and Logos" in *The Interpretation of History,* and also my essay on "Phänomenologie und Geschichte" in *Kairos* I (Darmstadt, 1926).

be so decisive for the form of grace which we hope we may yet witness, we may answer: the Catholic world has not taken the step which the Protestant world has taken, the step toward doing away with the objectification of the holy and the step toward a personal decision. The Catholic world must take this step; it cannot avoid it. It is not necessary that it follow the same path as Protestantism, but it must take this one step, the first and the decisive step. Nor is autonomous culture as such open to the coming of a form of grace. For it lacks a vital relationship to the sphere of transcendent meaning. To be sure, nothing is ever completely secularized. Indeed, there are within secularism so many points at which it is now breaking loose from its old moorings that perhaps the appearance of a new form of grace is better prepared for in this area than in ecclesiastical Protestantism, which still so largely clings to its traditional forms. If this be so, then Protestantism ought to be urged to take the step that will lead beyond its old forms just as Catholicism should be urged to take the step that Protestantism has already taken. To prepare the way—that is, first of all not to obstruct any form of grace that is united with radical prophetic criticism and with concrete rational criticism—to prepare the way into which the spirit of the Kairos and thus the principle of Protestantism will lead us: this is the task set before us, the task presented both to autonomous culture and to the Christian churches.

Religious Socialism*

1

The connection between religion and socialism in the concept "religious socialism" can be interpreted in very different ways. In each of these interpretations a certain *type* of religious socialism is revealed. In a systematic presentation it is necessary at the very beginning to clarify the way in which the term *religious socialism* is used, and to distinguish it from any other use.

a. The earliest, and therefore in many quarters the most telling, form of religious socialism is the *legalistic* one. It claims that socialism is the direct consequence of the moral demands of religion, especially of Christianity. To act according to the Christian commandment of love means to advocate socialism. The realization of socialism is the fulfillment of the Christian ethic. Such interpretations appeared particularly during the early stages of socialism. However, they are still effective even now, and often appear in the form of the claim that Jesus was the first socialist, and that adherence to his teaching must necessarily lead to the struggle on behalf of socialism. The legalistic type naturally shows sectarian traits. It is right in claiming an original historic and systematic connection between the commandment of love and the socialistic idea. It is wrong in the direct and unparadoxical way in which it establishes the connection.

b. The *romantic* interpretation represents the attempt to give

* Translated by William B. Green, Victor Nuovo and James L. Adams.

religious consecration to the present socialist movement. "Socialism *is* religion." Whoever participates deeply and actively in the socialist movement, in its community, in the shape that it gives to individual life, in its idea, in its impetus, in its readiness for sacrifice, in its certainty of victory—in just these things he possesses what is intended by religion. Socialism is his religion. The important truth that is basic to religious socialism is expressed by this interpretation, namely, that the religious principle is not confined to a specifically religious sphere. However, it is expressed in a way that renders it untrue. It overlooks the element of radical criticism that is inherent in every religion and which allows no actual realization of it to be exempt from criticism. The depth from which religion shakes every reality is covered up. One may ask: What is actually gained by calling socialism religion?

c. In contrast to this, the *practical-political* type of religious socialism attempts to unite the present socialist movement with the actual forms of religion, that is, with organized Christianity, with the churches. It is primarily concerned with the question of personal allegiance, with the possibility of being a socialist as well as a Protestant or Catholic Christian. The struggle of these Protestant or Catholic socialists is, therefore, directed against all those elements of socialism and of the churches which make personal allegiance impossible. This type of religious socialism has at present the widest and politically most effective representation. It is the necessary and meaningful expression of the concrete situation of numerous socialist Protestants and Catholics. But it is limited by its practical attitude. Because of this practical orientation, it does not always dig down deeply enough to the fundamental problems, and therefore it is unable to bring about a transformation of either religion or socialism from the deepest level.

d. This is the task of the fourth type of religious socialism, which may be characterized as *dialectical* or *dynamic*. It seeks to resolve the static opposition of the concepts of religion and socialism by demonstrating their dialectical relationship. It does not accept the inherited, empirical forms of religion and socialism as fixed and final, but rather attempts to understand them in terms of their elemental roots, and thus, to transform them. This type of religious socialism

is distinguished by its emphasis on theoretical problems. In contrast
to this, its practical effect is small. The following systematic outline
is presented from this standpoint.

2

a. Religious socialism is a phenomenon that was born of the
union of Christianity and humanism, a union rich in tensions. It is a
manifestation of *Christian humanism.* Humanism is Christian when
the universal and rational forms of that which is human are supported by a Christian substance *(Gehalt).* There is no such thing as
humanism in general and therefore no simple opposition between
Christianity and humanism. Just as the humanism of antiquity is
not humanism in general, but Greek humanism that is supported
by the substance of Greek paganism, so in socialism Christian and
humanistic elements are united from the beginning.

b. And yet the sharpest *opposition has arisen between Christianity
and socialism.* And this for two reasons: first, because humanism has
cut itself off from its religious background and from its intrinsically
religious origins; that is to say, it rejected the transcendent orientation *(profanisierte),*[1] and since an empty humanistic form does not
exist, it opened itself in this way to anti-Christian elements. The
second reason has to do with the situation in the Christian churches.
Having in part become fixated upon their prehumanistic forms, and
having also in part adapted themselves to profane humanism, the
churches were at the same time conditioned by the anti-Christian
spirit that had infiltrated them. Thus they came to be in opposition
to socialism in a double sense. So far as it is humanistically founded,
socialism opposes the preoccupation of orthodoxy with prehumanistic symbols. So far as it contains Christian elements, it
fights against the anti-Christian substance with which the profane
humanism and, along with it, the churches were to a large extent
imbued. Conversely, socialism experiences the rejection of the

[1] For Tillich's explication (on the basis of German usage) of the difference
between the terms *profane* and *secular* see his *Systematic Theology.* Three
volumes in one. (Chicago: The University of Chicago Press; New York: Harper &
Row, 1967), III, 87-89. "The term 'profane' in its genuine meaning expresses
exactly what we call 'resisting self-transcendence'. . ." (p. 87). Ordinarily, the
term *secular* is more neutral in this respect. (Tr.)

churches, on the one hand because of its profane-humanistic and anti-Christian elements, and on the other because of its attack on that form of humanism to which the churches were receptive. The situation is therefore very ambiguous and is accessible only to a dialectical analysis. In face of this situation any simple opposition or correlation of religion and socialism is completely inadequate.

c. Bourgeois society is the bearer of Christian humanism from its religious origins down to its profanely antireligious and anti-Christian realization. It is a social group with specific sociological qualities. Its decisive negative characteristic is its disavowal of any feudal-hierarchical obligations. Its decisive positive characteristic is its intention to achieve a rational understanding and control of nature and society.

The following stages of the development of bourgeois society are decisive for the basic attitude of religious socialism: (1) the anti-demonic, theocratic background of bourgeois society; (2) its disengagement from this background and its reorientation toward the finite and profanization; 3) the autonomous and rational realization of its principle; (4) bourgeois society's materialistic and idealistic interpretations of the situation; (5) the romantic counter-movements against it and their partial reception by it; (6) the revolutionary countermovements against it. Socialism belongs to this last stage. It was decisive for the history of socialism, particularly of German socialism, that it achieved its particular form simultaneously with its opposition to the idealistic interpretation of bourgeois society and also with its opposition to the romantic struggle against the bourgeois spirit: that is, it realized its form in Marxism. Sociologically, this led to the rejection by the proletariat of the bourgeois and feudal powers that had formed an alliance in Germany; with respect to religion, it led to the utilization of the materialistic-revolutionary interpretation of bourgeois existence, in opposition to the idealistic-progressive as well as the romantic-revolutionary conception of religion. Of the two elements of the bourgeois spirit socialism adopted one of them, the materialistic-revolutionary element, and turned it against the other, the idealistic, element which preserved a prebourgeois interpretation. This adoption of the materialistic element of bourgeois society led to the struggle between religion and socialism, which was characteristic of the German situation until the war [World War I], and among wide circles of both groups until the present. The intrinsic opposition of Christianity to the spirit of bourgeois society was hardly felt. Idealistic-romantic interpretations served to conceal the gulf between them. All the more emphatically did Christianity reject socialism when the latter openly revealed that opposition.

d. *The conquest of the opposition* between religion and socialism was possible only if two conditions were met: (1) provided socialism freed itself not only from the idealistic but also from the materialistic interpretation of bourgeois society—provided therefore that it grasped the opposition of religion and socialism more deeply and more radically than had generally been done during the nineteenth century; (2) provided that Christianity freed itself from the romantic-feudal as well as from the idealistic-bourgeois form of its realization, and thus more deeply and more radically understood its own nature as well as its freedom from every form, including even its own.

e. On the *religious* side, this latter course was taken by religious socialism in connection with the movement led by the Blumhardts. The *dialectical* type of religious socialism originates with them. The decisive idea of religious socialism is that religion does not have to do with a specific religious sphere but with God's dealing with the world, and that therefore it is possible that God's activity may be more clearly seen in a profane, even anti-Christian, phenomenon like socialism than in the explicitly religious sphere of the church. This led to the discovery of the possibility of an alliance between religion and socialism at a deeper level than the one on which they remained hopelessly opposed. In Germany, theological considerations in particular led to an insight into the inner dialectic of religion, and made possible a theological foundation for religious socialism.

On the *socialistic* side, the effect of the bourgeois youth movement, itself opposed to the spirit of bourgeois society, was to break up the soil among the younger generation of socialists and to challenge sharply the materialistically hardened dogmatism of the official party. Also, there was an increase in the number of bourgeois intellectuals who joined the socialist movement and offered resistance to the coarsened bourgeois spirit which, in part, they discovered in the socialist movement itself. In this they could appeal to Marx inasmuch as he represented a principle of dialectical thinking which was radically opposed to the dogmatic materialism of the nineteenth century. The dialectical type of religious socialism was founded by individuals who stood in the religious and socialist dialectic we have described.

It is unnecessary here to trace the intellectual history of the other types of religious socialism. The *practical-political* type has not yet offered an independent theological and sociological theory. It has in part adopted dialectical elements; in part, it expresses itself legalistically—especially in political propaganda. The purely *legalistic* type is rarely represented, and even then more by isolated individuals than by groups. Its roots are more typological than historical. The [*romantic*] type which identifies religion and socialism seems, finally, to have found a soil that has been intellectually and historically prepared for it in Russia. It is true that Bolshevism opposes the concept of religion; but in all its utterances it sets itself subjectively and objectively in the place of religion. Therefore, it must be interpreted—to be sure, against its will—as the foremost representative of the identifying type.

3

a. The opposition between religion and socialism appears, first of all, in their respective *conceptions of man*. This leads to an ambiguous state of affairs: insofar as socialism follows the typically bourgeois interpretation of man in its idealistic as well as in its materialistic form, it is opposed to Christian anthropology. On the other hand, insofar as it opposes the bourgeois conception, it represents decisive motifs of the Christian doctrine of man although in a very effective disguise. This ambiguity in the conception of man has already appeared in Feuerbach, to whom socialism owes its anthropological basis. The doctrines of Feuerbach about the limitlessness of human drives, about the formation of religious ideas by means of the projection and objectivization of the contents of these drives, form the basis of the Marxist concept of ideology. However, in place of man in general, Marx substituted historically determined man, that is, man determined by the class situation. This substitution, to be sure, was not radical. For in order to discuss the formation of society by means of the class struggle, Marxism must presuppose a universally human characteristic, on whose basis man, in spite of all his variations, is again and again driven to the formation of classes and, finally, beyond the class situation.

The conception of man underlying these ideas is subjected to a threefold evaluation by religious socialism: (1) The assessment of man implied in the concepts of projection and ideology is unconditionally affirmed. Every prophetic religion is inherently suspicious of religion that is based on man's wishes, of the "self-made God" [Luther], and of the unconscious use of the divine in the service of the will to power. This protest [against false religion] is powerfully expressed in the Feuerbach-Marxist theory of ideology. Religion must adopt this constant suspicion of ideology and apply it to itself. The Feuerbach-Marxist anthropology is useful to this end. (2) The materialistic form of the Feuerbach-Marxist anthropology emphasizes, on the one hand, the seriousness of its anti-idealistic protest, and to this extent (including its use of the term *historical materialism*) it is affirmed by religious socialism. On the other hand, religious socialism rejects materialistic doctrine as an interpretation of the bourgeois mechanization of the world. (3) In accord with the deepest motives of Feuerbach-Marxist anthropology, religious socialism rejects the idealistic element contained in Marxist anthropology, namely, the expectation that human nature will be transformed and completely subjected to the idea of justice. However, the prophetic element of Marxist anthropology, namely, the relatedness of man's being to a transcendent principle that is unconditionally valid and fulfilling is affirmed, along with the prophetic-revolutionary background of capitalism and socialism.

In summary, it can be said that religious socialism adopts the decisive intention of Marxist anthropology and radicalizes it by shedding those elements of Marxism which are derived from bourgeois materialism or idealism.

b. The anthropology of religious socialism seeks a basis that lies beyond the opposition between the materialistic and the idealistic conceptions of man. It has a dual starting point: namely, *the unity of that which is vital and spiritual* in man, and the simultaneous *disruption of that unity* which is the source of the threat to man's being. The following outline of the religious-socialist assessment of the situation of man in himself and in society proceeds from this dual point of view regarding the unity and the disruption of the vital and the spiritual: (1) In the light of the unity of the vital and the spiritual, of being and meaning, we can understand the proletarian situation as a situation in which man is radically threatened. The loss of a meaningful and vital mode of existence in the typically proletarian situation points to the threat to, and the reality of the loss of, meaningful existence. In the face of meaninglessness in the vital dimension of existence there is no validity in the demand on the part of the church or of a philosophical idealism for compensation in a spiritual world separated from that dimension. For the proletarian situation (we omit here the individual, heroic exceptions), the shattering of the meaning of life in the vital dimension amounts to the shattering of the meaning of life in general. For man is a unity of body and soul, and the meaning of his existence cannot be separated from the meaning of his bodily existence. In this view religious socialism represents the original intentions of the Old and the New Testaments. It overcomes in the same way the idealistic and the materialistic separation of the vital and the spiritual aspects of man's being. (2) The disruption of the unity of the spiritual and the vital leads to a view of man which sees him in the light of the essential threat to his existence, a threat that never disappears. Therefore, this view rejects every utopia, that is, every expectation of perfection within history. The disruption of man's unity (which does not thereby become a duality), a disruption belonging to man's being as spirit, signifies for man as man the threat of the loss of his being and his meaning. This threat is a *reality* and remains a reality as long as man is man. Religious socialism therefore takes account of this man in every structuring of society, and from it draws consequences that define its ethical position (see below, section 5, p. 51). (3) The question regarding a source of support corresponds to, and is as radical as, the radically threatened condition of man as man. For precisely this reason the support cannot arise from the human situation, but originates from that which is beyond man's being and its brokenness, from beyond being and freedom, and beyond the vital and the spiritual. In the relatedness of man's being to that which is beyond being and free-

dom, religious socialism discerns the root of the prophetic-eschato-
logical element in socialism (as well as in the original bourgeois-
idealistic utopianism). Since historical time, namely, a relatedness to
a transcendent fulfillment of meaning, is characteristic of man's
being, religious socialism supports the world-forming and world-
transforming intention of socialism. Here it also remains faithful
to biblical motifs in opposition to cultic conservatism.

4

a. Religious socialism stands fundamentally on the ground of
Marx's analysis of capitalistic society. This means: (1) It recognizes
that the structure of contemporary society is determined by the capitalist economy; that the market is the structural center of this economy
and society; and that the areas bordering the market, even when
they go beyond the market quantitatively (which is less and less the
case), are structurally secondary. This is true for all varieties of
prebourgeois social structure. With the advent of bourgeois society,
the latter have become antiquated and are not directly relevant for
the understanding of the present or for the shaping of the future.
(2) Religious socialism agrees with Marx that within capitalist
society there is a necessary opposition between the owners of the
means of production and those who are dependent upon these
means. Because it expands to include education and one's fate in life,
this opposition creates the differentiation of classes, which is in-
extricably connected with the capitalist structure, and in which
everyone participates objectively, whether or not he is aware of it
subjectively. (3) The class struggle is the necessary result of the differentiation of classes. According to the view of religious socialism,
the class struggle represents a structural necessity in capitalist society,
regardless of the good will of the individual. Therefore, it cannot
be interpreted as a matter of individual judgment. It is a fate that
no one can escape in face of the collision and incoordination of
interests in liberal society. (4) Out of the structure of capitalism
and the class struggle that is inherent in it arises the marked
tendency to overcome the form of society on which that structure
depends. This tendency can be represented dialectically, according
to Marx, in the economy as well as in all other areas. Religious

socialism, however, in agreement with Marx's original ideas, denies that dialectic is a mere calculation of necessities. It knows that in history fate realizes itself through freedom, and that without the bearers of the socialist fate, socialism can never become a reality. (5) Along with Marx, religious socialism sees in the proletariat the place given by fate for resistance to the capitalist structure of society. Therefore, it allies itself with the proletarian movement, whose political expression is essentially to be found in the socialist parties. Religious socialism is also aware of the fact, however, that the disposition of the proletariat by fate cannot be subject to calculation, and therefore can be lost. (6) The agreement of religious socialism with Marx's sociological analysis of capitalism does not as a matter of course imply its assent to his economic theory. Religious socialism takes no position whatsoever with respect to this theory. It is only of the conviction that theoretical analysis and the changing situation will lead beyond Marx, just as Marx led beyond the bourgeois economy. Socialism depends neither upon a specific economic theory nor upon the realization of *one* specific form of economy. For it, the only essential thing is the coming of an economy in which the lack of coordination of the forces and counterforces in capitalism is overcome, and through which the possibility of a meaningful society is given. And what is true for the end is true also for the means. It is not the task of religious socialism to solve concrete economic and political problems. It can, however, influence their solution indirectly by means of its total position.

b. This analysis of the structure of capitalist society, in connection with its statements about the human situation, leads religious socialism to the following interpretation of the present social situation from the perspective of the sociology of religion: (1) Bourgeois society as the bearer of Christian humanism is a form of the development of Christianity which stands in a dialectical relationship to the inner-religious forms of Christianity. In Christian humanism, an inner-religious realization of Christianity is transformed into an extra-religious autonomous one. On the one hand, this has led to liberation from the demonizations of the inner-religious sphere; and on the other, to an emptying-out of the originally religious substance and to vulnerability to extra-religious, profane demonizations. (2) Religious socialism perceives in the capitalistic system the cen-

tral demonization founded upon Christian humanism and upon
bourgeois society that represents it. Religious socialism calls the
capitalistic system demonic, on the one hand, because of the union
of creative and destructive powers present in it; on the other, because of the inevitability of the class struggle independent of subjective morality and piety. The effect of the capitalist system upon
society and upon every individual in it takes the typical form of
"possession," that is, of being "possessed"; its character is demonic.
The possibility that it may ally itself with other, in part more in-
digenous or primitive, demonries (for example, with nationalism
whose behavior is more expressly pagan) does not qualify its decisive
significance for the present situation. (3) Religious socialism believes
that its most decisive religious task in behalf of the present society
is to participate in exposing and combating a demonic capitalism.
Accordingly, it allies itself with the struggling proletariat whose
original vocation for this struggle it acknowledges. At the same time,
however, it knows that the proletariat may lose its "calling," hence
it directs a radically religious criticism against the profanizations
and demonizations occurring within socialism itself. (4) In the
struggle *against* a demonized society and *for* a meaningful society,
religious socialism discerns a necessary expression for the expectation of the kingdom of God. But it repudiates the identification of
socialism with the kingdom of God just as it rejects religious indifference towards constructive tasks within this world. It regards the
unity of the socialist dialectic, a unity of expectation and demand
of that which is to come, as a conceptual unity and at the same time
as a concrete and contemporary transformation of the Christian
eschatological tension. Yet it is aware of the uncertainty of every
concrete expectation and also of the distance that separates every
concrete realization from the intended unconditional fulfillment.
Therefore, it does not succumb to the profound disillusionment that
necessarily accompanies any uncritical (*ungebrochenen*) concrete
expectation of the end.

5

Certain basic ethical ideas follow from the religious anthropology
and sociology of religious socialism. They will be considered here

only insofar as they are essential to the structure of religious–socialist thought.

a. With respect to the action of the individual, (1) Religious socialism maintains that the age-old eudaemonistic theory, which makes the greatest possible increase of pleasure into a moral principle, must be rejected. It also rejects the heroic-idealistic theory which demands that the individual be subjected to an abstract law that is beyond and above man. The unity of being and meaning signifies just this, that even the most immediate instinctive drives possess an inclination toward the meaningful, and conversely, that the inclination toward the highest forms of meaning is still supported by instinctive impulses. This view at the same time serves to refute the conception of ideology which interprets man's action mechanistically according to the psychological principle of association and which regards sense perception as the primary psychic reality, tracing everything else back to it, and resolving everything from that point. In reality, every sensation is an *element* of a total event which can be reached only by means of a difficult process of abstraction. The spiritual, also, with all of its many tendencies, cannot for a moment be conceived apart from the total event. Religious socialism rejects as unsocialistic a socialist ethic that adheres to this bourgeois-positivist idea and which supplements it with an idealist morality. (2) The ethic of religious socialism, like its entire outlook, is dynamic. It does not recognize an abstract system of values that is universally valid but, rather, it discerns as an attribute of being itself a demand that changes according to the nature of the encounter between man and another entity. This demand can be fulfilled or it can be neglected; it is always concrete. Abstract value systems are exposed as the ideologies of ruling groups who instinctively want to give eternal sanction to their power by ascribing an eternal and transcendent character to their ethic. In place of this, religious socialism posits devotion to the dynamic meaning and its demands that are inherent in things and in situations. (3) The educational task of guiding the individual to meaningful structures to which he can devote himself arises out of the unity of being and meaning. The individual is not to be given an abstract or formal education, but is to become concretely involved in the meaning of all that he encounters. This presupposes the existence of such structures of meaning. Therefore, the presupposition of education is a meaningful social structure and institutions that make this devotion possible for the individual. On this basis, religious socialism is critical of the loss of meaning which has occurred in the human and material relationships within the capitalist system. (4) In the light of the brokenness of man's being, religious socialism rejects every utopian ethic. That man is good and that only social circumstances make him bad is as a generalization as false as it may be relatively true for a concrete situation, for example, the capitalist situation. The threat to man's being does not disappear even in the most perfect institution. The dynamic realization of every being always carries with it the possibility of doing violence to another. Just because being is dynamic, because it is daring and not mechanistic, it has this possibility. The devotion that is demanded by the meaning of what is encountered can fail to materialize. This holds for every order of society and is the basis of every socio-ethical and political theory.

  b. Religious socialism rejects the abstractly egalitarian and anarchist theory of the construction of society. It believes that even the history that Marx calls "prehistory" continues even in a classless society. Even here, in the classless society, there are tensions belonging to the intrinsic power (*Mächtigkeit*) of any existing thing that realizes itself dynamically and which exercises force and experiences force. This gives rise to the problem of power which socialist theory has almost always neglected on account of its liberal-anthropological basis. Religious socialism holds that the togetherness of all things, even in the coming society, will not persist in the polarity of power and love: power as the self-realization of the individual as well as of the group; love as devotion to the meaning of the self-realization of another. From these observations the following points of view result which help to clarify the socio-ethical and political thought of religious socialism: (1) The construction of society is necessarily a structuring of the levels of intrinsic power. This applies to the inner structure of nations as well as to the relation of nations to each other. The attempt to escape from this reality, as the history of democracy has shown, gives rise to concealed-power groups whose power is destructive because it is without responsibility (for example, in the domination exercised by capital). (2) Power is ultimately founded upon the recognition, for the most part unconscious, of the surpassing power of being of another. Power carries with it the possibility of oppression that trespasses beyond any legitimate recognition, and thus undermines it. In contrast to anarchist utopianism, the conceptions of power which isolate it and reveal an intoxication with it (Fascism) are based upon the confusion between power and the possibility of oppression. They forget that the foundation of power, namely the recognition of the surpassing powerfulness of those who bear it, is destroyed along with the breakdown of concern for the concrete meaning of the being of another. Groups that have lost their power may be able, by virtue of objective institutions of power, to exercise oppressive force for a little while longer, but their real power is destroyed along with the loss of recognition at the hands of the other. From this comes the objective and moral necessity for revolutionary action if occasion arises. For this reason religious socialism rejects the antirevolutionary dogma of Lutheranism, just as it regards its biblical foundation as also entirely false. (3) Recognition of legitimacy and concern for the meaning of the other presuppose a comprehensive principle of meaning. A group in which such a principle exists may be called a *community*, provided that all subjective and romantic features are removed from this concept. The development of a meaningful society, in which the possibility exists to recognize the meaningful power of being of another, or, what amounts to the same thing, the formation of a community as the unity of power and love, is the socio-ethical ideal of religious socialism. (4) From the basic anthropological idea of religious socialism as well as from its theory of intrinsic power (*Mächtigkeit*) and objective power (*Macht*) a wide range of implications emerge which have bearing on the theory of justice and the state and which lead far beyond the basic liberal scheme that socialism accepted uncritically from the bourgeoisie. Thus, religious socialism adopts tendencies that go back to Nietzsche, among others, and which at present are advocated exclusively by antisocialist groups. It believes that on the basis of a more profound conception of man, the legitimate motifs that are revealed there can be adopted by socialism and can be brought to realization in a form from which the demonic element has been removed.

6

The theological presupposition of religious socialism is the radical application of the prophetic-Protestant principle to religion and Christianity. This means: (1) A dialectical attitude toward one's own confessional form of religious life. The confessional character of every concrete religion is affirmed, and it is not abandoned in favor of a rational supraconfessionalism. The radical character of the religious principle, however, forbids a confessionalism that considers itself absolute. Therefore, it establishes a point within the system of every confession at which it transcends itself and opens itself to the meaning of the other confessions. It is true that this is a specifically Protestant formulation. But it stems from just that element of Protestantism in which the latter is not a confession. Therefore, religious socialism is not bound to a confession. It does not encroach upon the concrete confession of the individual; and for this reason it calls itself religious, and not Christian, Catholic, or Protestant socialism. (2) The dialectic of the religious principle frees it from bondage to the religious sphere as a sphere apart and creates in it an openness for the religious understanding of the profane. This point is decisive for laying the groundwork of religious socialism. For on this basis it is possible to present a religious analysis of the secular forms of socialism and to point out that, aside from their literal meaning, they are an expression, on the one hand, of the human situation in general and, on the other, of a particular situation in the context of the history of religion and the church. Religious socialism does not abandon the theoretical and practical forms of socialist life to their apparent secularity, but penetrates to the religious character of their basis. It points out, for example, that the basic Marxist concepts do not, in the consciousness of the socialist proletariat, have the character of a problematic science but that of a dogmatic symbol; that for the proletarian the party is not only a political group which he joins for reasons of expediency, but that it is also a fated community that supports him and has the character of a congregation for him; that the expectation of a classless society is the secular symbol for a religious, eschatological expectation; and that certain patterns of life of the socialist movement show the beginnings of a cultic institution, etc. Religious socialism also points to the ambiguity of these latently religious symbols and to the dangers resulting from them. (3) Conversely, religious socialism also undertakes a dialectical analysis, in terms of the religious principle, of the existence and of the practical and theoretical forms of life within the church. It points to the "profanity" in which all religious reality stands, solely by virtue of the fact that it is a concrete, historical reality. Therefore, it cooperates with the depth-psychological and sociological analyses of the forms of religious life within the churches, not in order to dissolve them, but rather to make them understandable in terms of their concreteness and dynamic, and thus to give them flexibility. This applies also to dogma, ritual, and church constitution, as well as to ethical insights. Only through the radical recognition of the unmediated profanity of these forms is the dialectical character of their religious meaning revealed. (4) The dialectical character of the religious principle solves the problem of the relationship between the will to transcend the world and the will to shape it. Religious socialism has used the New Testament word *kairos* for the solution of this problem. When used in this way Kairos signifies that the shaping of the world and of society is an inevitable consequence of the religious principle, but that this giving of form is not to be interpreted abstractly or in a utopian fashion. Rather, it is to be interpreted concretely and supported by that which is expected at some time to be fulfilled. Kairos always appears when temporal forms are in need of transformation and an eternal meaning is imminent, waiting to break through in temporal fulfillment. The extent to which this happens, that is, the degree to which a certain time is inwardly shaken, determines the power and depth of a Kairos. Religious socialism holds that the shaking of bourgeois society, of its spiritual and social principles, represents such a Kairos. And it attempts to hear and to obey the demand contained within it. (5) Theonomy is the goal of the creation of new form out of the Kairos. This concept also follows from the dialectic of the religious principle. Theonomy is a protest against an ostensibly realistic and religiously indifferent culture. It maintains that there can be cultural forms that resist being filled with transcendent import, and that there are others that open themselves to it and become pointers to and manifestations of a transcendent meaning. Religious socialism believes that the nature of profanized bourgeois society is such that it resists transcendence. It also holds that the shaking and transforming of that society points the way to a new theonomy in social and spiritual life.

7

a. Religious socialism is not bound to any sociological form. Its bearers can be individuals, labor groups, churches, or political groups. It can be organized independently, and it can represent the tendency of an existing organization. But it must be said of every one of its realizations that since it is aware of the dialectical character of the religious principle, it cannot assign absolute claims to any religious or politcal group, not even itself. Its task is to drive religion and socialism alike to their own depth and thus to point up their ultimate as well as their concrete unity, and to realize [this unity] in reality. To do this, it must work through both religion and socialism, church and party. It must be allied with both and critical of both.

b. The scope of the problems posed by religious socialism is universal. It touches upon all areas of economic, social, and spiritual life and attempts to influence them, on the one hand, in terms of the religious principle and, on the other, with regard to the present social reality. Thus it is by no means one-sided in its orientation, either politically or economically. It knows that the theonomous order of society to which it aspires must include all aspects of man's being, in order to fulfill only one part in terms of its meaning. For this reason, it is not bound to any economic theory or to any mode of political action. Whether socialist economic theory as it has developed up to the present, whether Marxism especially, is adequate for discerning the future of economic development is from the perspective of religious socialism a matter of indifference. Whether the present socialist parties are adequate bearers of the socialist idea or will remain such cannot be decided in advance, any more than the question of whether the proletariat will continue to be the most important bearer of the antidemonic struggle. This question remains open, as does the question of which church, if any among the contemporary churches, will serve as the basis upon which the unity of

religion and socialism can be realized. The idea of religious socialism is not affected by any of this. And yet the fact remains that
religious socialism, for the present, stands on the side of concrete
socialism and of its parties and therefore on the side of the
struggling proletariat. The radicalism of the religious principle does
not transcend entirely or do away with the concreteness of the
actual situation at hand.

Considered in terms of church history, religious socialism is an
attempt to unite the radical nature and the transcendence of the
religious perspective with the concreteness of an immanent will to
shape the world. It attempts to transcend (1) an exclusive Protestantism that sacrifices the concrete creation of form to religious transcendence, (2) a humanistic piety that sacrifices the radical nature of
the religious principle to the concrete creation of form, (3) a pietistic
inwardness that sacrifices the social *obligatum religiosum* to the
reservatum religiosum, (4) a hierarchical Catholicism that betrays
the concrete situation with the aid of a sacrosanct ethic possessing
metaphysical and sacramental sanctions.

In conclusion, it must be emphasized, in view of all that has been
said here, that religious socialism stands at the beginning of its development and has neither theoretically nor practically found its
definitive form.

Basic Principles of
Religious Socialism*

My task is to present a systematic summary of our convictions. What has been said in the preceding lectures should be understood, elaborated, and arranged from a single perspective. A system, however, is an individual creation. Therefore, a topical summary cannot be intended here but, rather, an independent construction that comprehends anew and from within all the problems dealt with. Only the unity of the ultimate goal with conclusive attempts at a solution is preserved. If this unity is authentic, it must prove to be so immediately in the creative systematic act itself.

Four trains of thought will be developed here in succession. We shall inquire about the inner attitude, the goal, the opponent, and the way of religious socialism.

1. THE INNER ATTITUDE OF RELIGIOUS SOCIALISM

We shall begin by making a distinction between two basic attitudes toward any actual situation: the sacramental attitude that lacks historical consciousness, and the rational attitude that is historically critical. The sacramental attitude is defined by a consciousness of the presence of the divine, be it in the primitive consecration of everything real or in the fixation of the holy upon

* Translated by James L. Adams and Victor Nuovo.

certain objects and actions. Here lies the root of sacred symbols and forms, of the sacred relationships of community and justice. On this basis we may explain the inviolable connections between man and the soil, between present and past generations, between rulers and the ruled, and between communities based on blood, folk, and race. All of these relationships are founded sacramentally regardless of the occasions that have led to their sacramental consecration. They owe to this character their power, endurance, and invulnerability, but at the same time they also owe to it the abundance of life, which they mediate, and the meaning of life, which they reveal. Here history is viewed as myth. It points out the occasions that have led to sacramental consecration, it contains the divine deeds upon which the import and the value of the present are based. There can be no doubt that even today there are still wide circles, especially of the peasantry, which are unaware of history, and that the sacramental spiritual situation is constantly strengthened by attachment to the soil despite the ongoing influence of the critical spirit. It is a great error if, from the perspective of the urban spiritual situation, one overlooks this fact, and, above all, if one does not grasp its metaphysical claim and its significance for every social structure.

The opposing spiritual situation derives not from import and consecration but, rather, from form and law (*Recht*). There is form and law in the sacramental attitude also, but they do not appear as form. It is directed not toward the right (*das Richtige*) but toward the holy (*das Heilige*), which may agree with the right but may also contradict it. On the other hand, in the rationally critical attitude, the holy that is not at the same time right and formed (*Richtige and Geformte*) is rejected. Spirit is directed toward form and thereby loses the presence of the holy. It becomes separated from everything given and becomes empty and without import. It pursues the unconditioned pure form *ad infinitum* without being able to find it. This critical rational spirit is the genuine heritage of the primitive wanderlust in social conditions that issue from an uprooting from the soil, as in colonies and cities. It is the titanic world-forming will that wants to restore the lost presence of the holy through the creation of form. But this will, from which flows all the creative activity of the spirit, breaks down because of the loss that it necessarily brings about. The holy that is given cannot be replaced by the holy that is demanded. Reflection, creative activity, is endless and is emptied of all that is present in favor of a future that is never realized. This is the tragedy of all reflection, that by itself it necessarily deepens the gulf that separates it from reality, and which it desires to overcome. It is the barrenness of every reflective attitude toward the present that it not only cannot create the future it demands, but it also hinders its coming. Whereas it is hardly necessary in our circle to be critical of the sacramental, unhistorical conception, it is necessary to point out the danger of rational criticism. Numerous contemporary critical movements share the fate of reflection and its sterility, even though they fly from reflection into subjective feeling, as, for example, in the case of the youth movement. The one can create import or meaning (*Gehalt*) as little as the other, for both stand on the same ground of subjective detachment from the immediacy of the holy and its unconditionally meaning-fulfilling power.

In contrast to both of these tendencies, religious socialism adopts the prophetic attitude. It is the unity and a higher form of both of the former tendencies. The demand of the holy that should be arises upon the ground of the holy that is given. Prophetism is neither mantic that predicts the future nor ethics that demands the future. Prophetism grasps the coming that should be from its living connection with the present that is given. It has the holy, but only as it permeates law and form; it is free from sacramental indifference, but it does not succumb to rational purgation. Prophetism is a religious and spiritual function that persists. It can be weaker or stronger, purer or more distorted, but never missing. It is the religious unity of morality and the metaphysics of history, and can be borne by individuals, groups, and movements, indeed, even by the masses. It is susceptible to error to the degree that it becomes mantic, and it is barren to the degree that it becomes moralism.

The prophetic attitude is essential to religious socialism. It exists in socialism even though it is frequently distorted by reflection, rationalism, and political strategy. Everything depends upon whether these elements in socialism are subordinated and its pure prophetic power becomes manifest. The fate of the socialist movement hinges upon the success or failure of this effort. Whether it proceeds from the prophetic attitude or not is decisive for all discussion about religious socialism. Every debate that remains only in the rational plane does not penetrate to the essence. The rational attitude necessarily misunderstands the prophetic. In this way bourgeois science refuted socialism, and the Enlightenment refuted the teachings of faith, successfully in the rational sphere while missing the essence itself. They did not reach the metaphysical and the ethical and their unity, namely, the prophetic element of those creations. Nevertheless, religious socialism should not underrate the rational element. It must radically affirm law and form precisely from its prophetic consciousness. It must demand correct form even more strongly than rationalism. But it must recognize that the presence of the Unconditional is the *prius* of all conditioned action, that the unconditioned import of meaning is the *prius* of all forms of meaning, that the development of form (*Gestalt*) is the *prius* of all form-creation (*Gestaltung*).

We have used the word Kairos for the content of the prophetic view of history. It signifies a moment of time filled with unconditioned meaning and demand. It does not contain a prediction of a nearer or more distant future; as far as it does involve this, mantics is joined to prophetism and the possibility of error to unconditioned certainty. But Kairos also does not signify a mere demand or ideal. As far as these are involved, it is discerned either as a momentary trend that is not reality, or as utopian. Kairos is the fulfilled moment of time in which the present and the future, the holy that is given and the holy that is demanded meet, and from whose concrete tensions the new creation proceeds in which sacred import is realized in necessary form. Prophetism is consciousness of Kairos in the sense of the words: "Repent; the time (*kairos*) is fulfilled and the kingdom of God is at hand."[1] Thus the sacramental and the critical attitudes are united in the consciousness of the Kairos, in the spirit of prophetism.

---

[1] Tillich quotes this line in Greek, conflating Matt. 4:17 and Mark 1:15, (Tr.) The reader will find a more extensive exposition of the key concepts of this and the following sections of the present essay, in Tillich's *Philosophy of Religion* (1925) which appears in *What is Religion?* ed., James L. Adams (New York: Harper & Row, 1969).

2. THE GOAL OF RELIGIOUS SOCIALISM

How are we to understand the "sovereignty of God"? The answer to this question must be given primarily and fundamentally as follows: it is the realization of unconditioned import in unconditioned form according to the saying "God is all in all." But this saying expresses an idea. It expresses the truth about the real, not reality itself. In reality we find a series of creative syntheses in which the eternal idea, the absolute synthesis, is revealed. One such concrete synthesis we call theonomy. It is the content of the prophetic view of history, the creation that is experienced in the Kairos simultaneously as given and as demanded (as near at hand). Theonomy is a condition in which the spiritual and social forms are filled with the import of the Unconditional as the foundation, meaning, and reality of all forms. Theonomy is the unity of sacred form and sacred import in a concrete historical situation. Theonomy transcends the indifference to form of the sacramental attitude of spirit in the same way as it transcends the emptying of import in formal autonomy. It fills the autonomous forms with sacramental substance. It creates a sacred and a just (*gerechte*) reality at the same time.

Theonomy is distinguished in like manner from both other-worldly and this-worldly utopianism. Otherworldly utopianism, the absolute rule of God as a concrete ideal, is usually associated with the sacramental attitude, whereas this-worldly utopianism, the perfect kingdom of reason, is associated with the critical attitude. Otherworldly utopianism is deeper, inasmuch as it sees the unity of form and import in the absolute sovereignty of God and therefore also conceives nature, the basis of all realization of form, as taken up into the condition of perfection. But it confuses idea and appearance, truth and reality. It makes the idea into a higher reality and places the Unconditional merely alongside the conditioned, thereby contradicting the essence of the Unconditional and devaluating the conditioned. Every theology that devaluates this world must be opposed not only from the socialist standpoint, but even more from the religious standpoint. Reality is the locus of the revelation of the Unconditional, in individual as well as in universal history. And no one and no time can have a greater share in the idea than it realizes in the phenomenon. This is the unconditional seriousness which belongs to the conditioned, in individual as well as in communal life. However, affirmation of this world does not imply an affirmation of this-worldly utopianism, which, rather, is to be rejected just as emphatically as otherworldly utopianism. It is more utopian than the latter, inasmuch as it leaves nature untouched and wishes to erect a rational social and spiritual structure on an irrational natural foundation. It forgets that the unconditioned form can never be realized as such, that it is an ultimate abstraction, a purely ideal point of direction, but it is not reality. Everything real, however, is the individually creative synthesis of universal form and of the irrational ground of nature. For everything real is concrete. Religious socialism is distinguished from utopianism by the fact that its goal is individually creative, born concretely in history. It desires theonomy, not a rational utopia. In theonomy, however, the individual, the concrete, and the creative are preserved, for import is united with form on the irrational ground of nature only in the creative individual.

The relation of theonomy to religion and culture follows directly from these definitions of the essence of theonomy. In an ideal theonomy, religion and culture cannot exist merely side by side. Every coordination of the Unconditional and the conditioned makes the Unconditional conditioned and the conditioned unconditioned. All culture is actualized religion, and all religion is actualized as culture. There can be no other expression for the direction of the spirit to the Unconditional than conditioned forms, and no other import can give meaning and reality to conditioned forms than the unconditioned meaning upon which they rest. The more a spiritual situation realizes this unity of form and import, the more it is to be characterized as theonomous.

But these definitions are not adequate. Theonomy realizes itself individually and creatively upon the irrational ground of nature from which it wrests its individual form-giving power. Where there is individual creativity, there is also opposition to the creative process and there are also forms that contradict form. We call the embodiment of these forms that oppose the unconditioned form and are therefore destructive and self-destroying, the demonic, in contrast to the unity of forms subjected to the Unconditional, that is, in contrast to the divine. In every culture we find divine and demonic forms intermingled. Consequently, a simple identification of religion and culture can never be asserted. Religion always has a dual relation to culture. It contains within itself a No, a *reservatum religiosum*, and a Yes, an *obligatum religiosum*. By virtue of the *reservatum religiosum*, the religious spirit falls back upon itself in the face of the demonically distorted and conditioned forms of an epoch; that is, it falls back upon the sacred personality and the sacred community in a strict sense. In this way, the culturally negative attitude of early Christianity, of mysticism in late antiquity, and of Lutheranism may be interpreted as a religious withdrawal (*Reservat*) before the predominance of the demonic in social, personal, and political life. This religious withdrawal can and must always come into force again; it is the ground for the delimiting of a sacred alongside a secular sphere. But it becomes false, and opens the way to the demonic as soon as it forgets the other side, the *obligatum religiosum*. In reality, religion is never able to do without cultural forms. In the most profound act of religious introspection, forms of cultural creation are operative. Moreover, the religious communities that renounce the world are themselves "world" in the forms of their renunciation and in their own life-forms. The *reservatum* without the *obligatum* is impossible and untrue. Just as untrue, however, is the affirmation of the *obligatum* without the *reservatum*, as is almost the case with autonomous Protestantism. To reduce religion to cultural activity is to forget that all culture lives from the Unconditional, which is intended in religion, and that, therefore, a culture religion not only dissipates religious substance but also robs culture of its import. Therefore, culture is right in renouncing culture-Protestantism, and religion is right in rejecting the identification of religion and socialism. The only proper attitude toward culture and also toward socialism is that characterized by the double demand of *reservatum* and *obligatum religiosum*.

The attitude of theonomy toward the churches and confessions also follows from what has been said. They are the representatives of the *reservatum religiosum*, and from this follows their positive and negative valuation: positive, inasmuch as they are the focal points of the religious spirit; negative, inasmuch as in their forms they are just as much culture as the secular culture that confronts them; positive, inasmuch as it is an impossibility and an error of the critically rational attitude to suppose that symbols can be made; negative, inasmuch as no symbol may make a claim to absoluteness. The churches with their cultic and mythical symbols are absolute neither toward each other nor toward the forms of secular culture. Every religion stands under the No issuing from the Unconditional. Therefore, the exclusiveness of confessionalism is abandoned, but not by criticism of confessionalism in general but, rather, by a deepening of the confession to the point where it negates itself before the Unconditional. Not skeptical and rational criticism, but only profound religious criticism can overcome the hubris of the confessions. Therefore, this ultimate negation before the Unconditional does not at all preclude an emphatic Yes in conditioned circumstances. In the empirically cultural sphere, confessional conflict has the same right as the conflict that prevails in all creative realms of spirit. But the creative, symbol-bearing conviction of the truth of one's own confession is not the same as the certainty of the Unconditional itself, which transcends the entire plane of convictions, even confessional ones. This conception of the duality of certainty and conviction with respect to every religious symbol is the presupposition for a religious consciousness of unity directed toward humanity. It is a consciousness that is far from a critical purgation of the confession and its individually creative symbols. Only a religion that includes in its own symbols this negativity toward itself has the power to become a world religion. The more it negates itself from the point of view of the Unconditional, the more justified a claim to absoluteness by a confession or a church, and the easier for religious socialism to enter into the symbols of such a church. But the No coming from the Unconditional is directed not only against itself as confession, but also against itself as a specifically religious sphere. Religion is truer the more it cancels itself out (*aufheben*) as religion over against culture without thereby losing its specifically religious power. Likewise it is truer the closer it stands to theonomy in which religious symbols are the ultimate and most universal expression of autonomous cultural consciousness, and in which autonomous culture-forms radiate the fullness of the import of the Unconditional. The closer a religion

stands to this ideal of theonomy, the more easily can an auton-
omously born religious socialism unite with it. For theonomy is
the goal of religious socialism.

3. THE STRUGGLE OF RELIGIOUS SOCIALISM

a. Basic Principles

Theonomy, as it is represented in the contemporary era, receives
its clearest expression through the understanding of what at present
opposes its realization. The goal of religious socialism becomes most
conspicuous through its struggle. Theonomy stands in opposition
to the predominance of the demonic. The struggle of a religious
movement can never direct itself against the secular or the irreli-
gious. The secular abides in the religious and has just as much reality
as there is religious substance within it. Rather, religion struggles
against antidivine religion, against the demonic. Therefore, a
profound and creative identification of the object of the struggle of
religious socialism must begin with a conception of the general
nature of the demonic, and proceed to an understanding of the
demonry of this Kairos.

The demonic is the contradiction of unconditioned form, an eruption of the irrational ground of any realization of form that is
individual and creative. The irrational can contradict unconditioned form only when it clothes itself in forms and opposes these
to unconditioned form. The demonic is never formless. In this
respect it is like the divine. It is also like it in the fact that it is
not reduced to form (that is, is not exhausted in it) but, rather,
filled with import, it bursts form open. The demonic, like the
divine, is perceptible in the ecstatic, the overwhelming, and the
dreadful. But whereas the ecstatic element of the divine affirms the
unconditioned form and therefore creates forms, the ecstatic element
of the demonic destroys form. We can distinguish between the
divine and the demonic by their relation to unconditioned form.

In the immediacy of the sacramental spiritual situation, the
divine and the demonic are mixed. We call theocratic the rising
of the divine against the demonic and the consequent dissolution

of sacramental immediacy. By this concept we do not mean the external appearance of a priestly or religious dominion but, rather, the will to conquer the sacred reality of the demonic in the name of sacred unconditioned form. It would not be difficult to show that the deepest root of even external theocracy is this inner theocratic tendency, which, to be sure, is often enough again misdirected into the demonic. In this sense, therefore, theocratic movements are antidemonic inwardly religious reform movements, like Jewish prophetism, Mohammedanism, monastic reform, Calvinism, and the socio-ethical sects. In this sense, religious socialism is also a theocratic movement.

The goal of theocratic movements is the sovereignty of the unconditioned form, of the right and the just. But as soon as this goal is reached, the danger threatens that sacred import will be lost. Formalism and emptiness always threaten. Form frees itself from sacramental constraint and from its fullness of import. It becomes profane or secular. Theocracy passes over into autonomy. Autonomy is able to elaborate pure forms with rational perfection in every sphere, but, by itself, it cannot bring about the fulfillment of forms in any sphere. It lives on the import of the past and the more it produces abstract forms, the more it becomes separated from life. A complete autonomy would mean the complete destruction of life. But life does not let itself be destroyed, and as the divine import of theonomy is dissipated, the demonic import that was previously subjected breaks forth from the life ground and uses autonomous form for the destruction of form. This resurgence of the demonic is characteristic of an era purged by autonomy. It is the peculiar form of reaction against the rising theonomy of our time. The result is a two-sided conflict of theonomy rising against the demonry of this Kairos. On the one side are the unconquered residues of the old sacramental demonry against which religious socialism must continue the theocratic conflict with the aid of autonomous forms. On the other side are the reappearances of the demonic which find their way into the empty space created by autonomous formal criticism, and which frequently strive for sacramental meaning by the use of autonomous forms. Between the two stands autonomous form. It stands over against both. Nevertheless, it can never be willed as form, but only as an expression of

import. The conflict of religious socialism is directed against
sacramental and natural demonries. Corresponding to the duality
of all form-giving power that creates either ideal or real forms,
either theoretical or practical forms, is the substratum of the realization of all forms, the irrational ground. It too can be conceived as
a duality: either as a drive to become one with being (*das Seiende*)
or as a drive to transcend being, either as will to abandonment or
as will to self-assertion. Love and power are polar opposites. Nevertheless, they are basically identical substrata of all creative form-
giving power. Therefore, they are the bearers of divine and demonic
ecstasy. Both primordial elements of the creative ground have always been recognized, and for the most part, one has been considered more worthy than the other: love above all by Plato, in
innumerable appearances of mysticism, in romanticism, and the
like; the will to power in voluntarism, in the philosophy of nature
of the Renaissance, in Boehme, Schelling, Schopenhauer, Nietzsche,
etc.; and both of them in realistic psychology and sociology, above
all in poetry, but also in science. Essential to a clearer view of these
two powers as symbols of the creative ground is their intrinsic
dialectical character, their capacity to break out into divine and
demonic ecstasy. Both powers are contained in every creative reality;
it is not possible to separate will-to-power from love or love from
will-to-power. Yet in every phenomenon one or the other can be
recognized more clearly. The dominion of pure form seeks to drive
out both. The perfected autonomy of form would create a rational
reality without the erotic and the dynamic. It would be without
the demonic, but also without divinity. However, no such reality
is possible, for the erotic and the dynamic powers are the real in
every actuality, forming its ground and its abyss. It would be a
misunderstanding if one tried to take these concepts, in the universal application that they are given here, strictly and objectively
in a psychological or sociological sense. One would thereby become
guilty of poor metaphysics. Rather, they are to be taken symbolically
as an expression of the creative ground that reveals itself with great
symbolic force through the phenomena designated by them. The
irrational ground they are supposed to symbolize is, however, no
longer logically but only metalogically conceivable.

The basic definitions have now been given with which it is

possible to approach an interpretation of the contemporary Kairos from the point of view of the Unconditional. In all spheres, religious socialism must lead the struggle against the demonries of the sacramental spiritual situation and against the natural demonry that emerges for the first time. In this struggle it must avail itself of pure rational form, offered to it by the autonomous culture of previous centuries. But, beyond that, it must strive for the revelation of a new sacred import by which autonomous form is fulfilled. In the conflict against sacramental and natural demonry, religious socialism adopts rational, liberal, and democratic elements. In the struggle for a new import it opens itself to the theonomous elements of past and present spiritual situations. In both cases, however, it seeks to eliminate the demonic elements: in liberalism and rationalism, the natural demonries that have entered in as a consequence of the process of purgation [by formal rationalism], in sacramentalism, the frequently hardened sacramental demonries that accompany it.

b. The Struggle in the Theoretical Sphere[2]

The systematics of science treats the structure of the spiritual functions. We shall extract from it the basic division into world-grasping and world-shaping functions, and, in each of the two groups, the division into functions that give conditioned meaning, and functions that are directed toward unconditioned meaning. Thus, in the theoretical sphere, we find science and art in contrast to metaphysics, and in the practical sphere, we find law and community in contrast to ethics. Moreover, a further distinction can be made between the functions of conditioned meaning: thus science and law are concerned more with form, art and community more with import.

In the sacramental spiritual situation there is a directedness toward unconditioned meaning, that is, toward the meaning that governs the import upon which all other meaning is founded. Logical and aesthetic forms express omnipresent import; they are affirmed for their power to express metaphysical intuition and not

---

[2] Cf. my book, *Das System der Wissenschaften nach Gegenstanden und Methoden* (Göttingen, 1923), reprinted in *Gesammelte Werke*, Vol. I (Stuttgart, 1959). [Cf., also James Luther Adams, *Paul Tillich's Philosophy of Culture, Science, and Religion*, Chap. III (New York: Harper & Row, 1965). Tr.]

for their autonomous value. Sacred science and sacred art create symbols for a basic metaphysical attitude. They are closely bound together and their uniform symbol is myth. Things have mythical, intrinsic, and special sacramental significance. But they are not things in a strict sense, they are essences with their own power and with their own erotic drive. Through eros and the will to power, spirit enters into relation with their innermost core.

But this sacramental significence of things deprives them of their formal significance. They are grasped not in their own forms, but in their metaphysical relation to eros and power. They are violated by eros. Sacred inviolability and absoluteness maintain distortions in logical as well as in aesthetic forms. The demonic force of such a sacred opposition to meaning is manifest in the subjection and destruction of spiritual freedom and creative power by which it holds nations and classes in subhuman bondage and apathy, and destroys every autonomous effort. The unconquerable fear of the demonic in things, the servitude of taboo and the broken consciousness of truth are the demonic effects of sacred opposition to form in the theoretical sphere.

The theocratic conflict must be continued against these forms of the demonic, which are a contemporary force in sacramental and orthodox confessionalism. Protestantism and the Renaissance began the conflict; the Enlightenment brought it to autonomous maturity. The coming theonomy must not lose the seriousness and the rigor of Kant's autonomous attitude, of the empirical sciences, and of classical-realistic art. As a champion of social justice, religious socialism must seek justice for things in the theoretical sphere, that is, the justice implicit in the affirmation of their proper forms, in their rational, logical, or aesthetic contexts.

So long as this struggle is carried on with the power of prophetic-theocratic import, it escapes the fate of purgation. It is supported by *eros* and *dynamis*, as in the great events of the Renaissance down to the seventeenth century. But as soon as this import disappears, nothing remains but the empty grandeur of autonomous form and the endless quest for scientific and artistic form. Then another erotic and dynamic power, different from the divine that drives toward the Unconditional, takes possession of this empty form.

The loss of intrinsic power and erotic drive to which things are subjected by rational science, somehow fails to come to an end in a system of formal relations that reveal their own abstract and merely formal character. Rather, a new fear of demons takes possession of these forms. There arises a belief either in meaningless necessity or in meaningless willfulness as the heart of things. In place of the meaningful framework of fate and in place of spiritual reality, whose highest form is creative freedom, there appears the demonic pair, necessity and chance. Whether in naturalism or naturalistic voluntarism, metaphysical as well as pragmatic, God always has demonic-ecstatic, meaning-destroying features. World-import and world-meaning become divided.

The cognitive attitude corresponds to the object of cognition. The critical rational moderation and the skeptical objectivity of science that is indifferent to import are used to promote a hubris of rationality that dissolves all that remains of sacramental immediacy. Now, however, a new irrational ground is sought to replace the lost metaphysical import. It is the subjective relationship of eros and power to things which supports the hubris of rationality. It is the exterior side of this relationship, that is, the place where things open themselves to subjective eros and to subjective will to power, which is turned toward the exterior side of the knower. It is the form of things accessible to technology and utility upon which the hubris of rationality is founded. Thus there arises a natural subjectivism that is like sacramental objectivism and has the same demonic consequences. For this dependence of the cognitive attitude upon subjective eros and the will to power, whose classical theoretical expression is pragmatism, signifies the breakdown of the meaning of knowledge, the isolation of the knower from the known, and the destruction of the universal organism of truth. Religious socialism, desiring a universal community in the social sphere, must also strive for the universal, living unity of knowledge. It must oppose the demonic subjectivity of pragmatism, not only in its liberal-individualistic, but also in its Marxist-sociological, form. It must leave things to their own form, to their own intrinsic power and erotic nature; it must restore them to destiny and freedom; and it must therefore break through the mechanized external aspect to the point where the universal context of cognition arises and with it a theonomous and not demonic metaphysical attitude. The *Gestalt* theory of knowledge, of creative fulfillment of meaning, and of metalogically dynamic method in philosophy are attempts to advance in this direction. They are ways to a new theonomy in cognition.

In the aesthetic sphere, the turning toward the intrinsic forms of things brings about a classically realistic trend. The demonic distortions of the hieratic style are overcome in favor of pure self-enclosed forms. The essence of the aesthetic as a peculiar function of meaning with its own norms becomes evident. Corresponding to the theocratically autonomous apprehension of the holy, mythical symbols are classically formed and raised into the aesthetic sphere. Myth loses its religio-metaphysical quality and becomes art. But classical realism is vital only so long as the mythical import is still operative in it. If this import is lost, a classical formalism results that, on its own part, is grasped by the subjective eros and the will to power and is used for new naturalistic, demonic creations. They are the subjective erotic, the impressionism, and the will to power of aesthetic distance that use aesthetic form to create a formless realism or the art of decadence at the point where they seize upon their own demonic essence. Thus, in the aesthetic sphere, a parallel creation to naturalism and pragmatism is achieved. In contrast, there are in the expressionist movement and in the new understanding of hieratic and primitive art tendencies leading toward a theonomous art filled with sacramental import. It is of highest importance for socialism, which must strive for symbols of a theonomous community, to participate in these movements and to attempt through metaphysical criticism to seek to protect them from succumbing again to subjectivism and aestheticism, as so often happens.

In both spheres of the theoretical fulfillment of meaning, the theonomous goal is an attitude in which autonomous forms, freed from sacramental distortion, are, in turn, freed from those naturalistically demonic distortions that enter in to empty them, and are filled with the import of the Unconditional. Genuine metaphysics is not theory and dogma; it is, rather, a tendency of the meaning-fulfilling spirit, a directedness toward the Unconditional. It is important to give to this tendency such an expression in science and art that both of them, without detriment to the autonomy of their forms, may, in a new alliance, create symbols of a new theonomous union of spirit and reality.

c. The Struggle in the Practical Sphere

1. In the sacramental spiritual situation, justice and community are directed toward the realization of the Unconditional. Community is cultural community and all social relations have sacramental consecration. Autonomous personality, and with it autonomous justice and autonomous society, have not yet appeared. The personality is completely dominated by sacramental relations to the soil, possessions, the family, the tribe, the class, the nation, and the politico-cultic hierarchy. It is enclosed within this system of material and personal relationships, which is cultically consecrated and which depends upon power and eros. From this system personality derives its import, its abundance, and its importance. But the system also hinders and interrupts its autonomous development. From it originate sacred acts of injustice, the demonic destruction and sacrifice of personality for the sake of relationships sacramentally consecrated to power and eros. The relationship to wife, child, slave, stranger, the member of a lower caste, the enemy, etc.; the subjection of the values of autonomous personality and of social relationships to the framework of one's own blood, tribe, and sex, and also the impairment of technological domination of the soil and of the rest of nature—these are all the consequences of the sacramental social attitude. Because of them the theoretical conflict against sacramentalism begins, namely, the struggle for justice and equality, the recognition of personality, and the emancipation from bondage to nature. Religious socialism must enter into this conflict, which was carried on most forcefully and successfully by Jewish prophetism; it must strive against all sacramental demonries, their feudal, agricultural and ecclesiastical residues. Moreover, it enters the conflict together with liberalism and democracy. The concept of human rights is for it no slogan but, rather, the symbol of the victorious conquest over social injustices and sacramental demonries.

But religious socialism also recognizes that empty forms of freedom and equality are abstractions and not realities; whenever the sacramental import of the social sphere has been lost on account of the victory of pure form, the subjective will of eros and power takes possession of this form and distorts it demonically. Religious socialism perceives the natural demonries that appear with the growing conquest of a rational form of society, and sees, as its main task, the combatting of this and the striving for a new import. We shall now consider this dual struggle against sacramental and natural demonries as it affects the spheres of economy, law, state, and community.

2. In the sacramental spiritual situation, the relationship to the soil and to other things is consolidated and mythically grounded. The powers of the soil and the divinities of other goods stand in a specially intrinsic relationship with the possessor. A sacred eros provides a basis for property and a sacred power sets men over things.

But, for this reason, things lose their special nature and their intrinsic power. Only under certain limitations and within narrow bounds is the use of things possible; beyond that the fear of taboo guards the special nature of things. The thing is not yet a thing, but therefore the person also is not yet a person. The concealed powers of things retard the development of personality with demonic force. Consequently, theocratic and rational movements always strive for an abrogation of the sacramental consecration of things and for an understanding of things according to their rational value. Things are deprived of their intrinsic power; they become rational economic instruments. This happens first to movable goods, primarily to those used for trading, that is, money, but finally to the immovable earth. With the rational thing-value which they acquire, things lose their cultic eros-value. The more a thing becomes a mere commodity, the less it exists in an eros-relation to the possessor and the less intrinsic power it possesses. In this inner emptiness, however, the thing becomes the object of the subjective eros and of the subjective will to power. The mere desire for pleasure and the infinite desire for domination take possession of things that have become commodities, and subject them to a degree that also eliminates the possibility of their intrinsic eros-relation, and they do this to an infinite degree. The subjective will to power that follows a rational course has no limit, but in order to be able to control the limitless, it must renounce its intrinsic import and sacrifice it to infinite activity that is empty. What it takes away from things it loses for itself, and it thus becomes a thing in the oppressive process of a limitless industrial economy. Natural demonry destroys personality precisely as did sacramental demonry.

At this point we take up the decisive problem of economic ethics, the problem of need. Emancipation from the limitless drive of a rational liberal industrial economy is possible only by transforming the eros-relation to things. Property itself cannot be debased, but only that property which has not become property in the sense of intrinsic power and eros-relation. Real property is limited by nature and is a necessary basis for personal power. In theonomy, need is based not upon demonic taboo, but upon a living eros-relation between person and thing. An industrial economy that would satisfy need in this sense must undergo a fundamental change. This is a goal of religious socialism, though it may be difficult to attain because population growth linked with a rational and limitless use of the world's resources is an obstacle that can only gradually be overcome.

The second decisive point in the consideration of industrial economy is the technological relationship of personality to things in the process of production. Every restriction of infinite technological exploitation of things falls together with the barriers of taboo. The rational aspect of things receives exclusive consideration together with the necessity that men accommodate themselves to it. The result is the mechanization of the process of production, whose symbol is the machine. The possibility of doing away with the machine is, of course, out of the question. The destruction of machines is merely an atavistic reversion to sacramental demonry and an acknowledgment that the taboo that obstructs technology is valid. Therefore, it can be only a matter of removing the mechanical element from the machine, which is, in truth, only one aspect of its nature. Intrinsically, the machine is an authentic *Gestalt* with individual holistic quality, a *Gestalt* that demands productive empathy and living eros. Therefore, not the mechanized but the living personality is adequate to the machine, although, in contrast to handicraft, only within certain very essential limits— limits that result from the necessary subordination to rational laws.

But even these limits can be extended and the individual tech-nological *Gestalt* can be raised far above handicraft in significance by adapting it to the universal framework of production. There can and must be a *mythos* of technology, and therefore also a cultic consecration of technological production, just as both exist for handicraft.

It follows from what has been said that religious socialism must establish anew a relationship between person and thing founded upon eros and power, by acknowledging the technological utiliza-tion of things; also by rejecting all frantic resentment of ma-chines as well as any flight to an idyll of handicraft, it must help to make effective an eros-relation between technological *Gestalt* and personality, and it must give mythical and cultic consecration to the universal, technological world-industrial process. In this way it expresses its opposition to romantic reaction as well as to the naturalistic demonic autonomy of industrial economy. In this way, too, the idea of a theonomous attitude toward industrial economy is posed.

3. The problem of an industrial economy must always be ap-proached from two sides: on the one side, the relation of person and thing comes into view; on the other, the relation of persons to each other. In most economic theories, the first side has been neglected. The limitless rational will to power in industry is held to be an obvious presupposition. The foregoing discussion has shown that this is by no means the case. However, it is necessary to complete the discussion from the other side.

In the sacramental spiritual situation, the relation of persons to each other is determined by the directly consecrated cultic com-munity. The demonic perversion of power and eros, that is, the subjection of personalities, is necessarily bound to sacramental im-mediacy. Consequently, the theocratic reaction against sacramental-ism strives for the emancipation of personality and—inasmuch as this emancipation affects everyone—for equal justice. Thereby jus-tice loses its immediate unity with social reality; it becomes formal and autonomous and comes under the categories of freedom and equality. The idea of the rights of man is the perfect expression of the theocratically rational tendency in the practical sphere. The demand that religious socialism assist in bringing the idea of absolute justice to radical fulfillment is self-evident. Here, religious socialism immediately joins religious, theocratic liberalism. Together with it, it must strive against the sacramental demonic powers that destroy personality—whether it be against the residues of sacramental demonry in European culture, or against Asiatic sacramentalism whose dominion remains unbroken.

With the victory of pure justice, however, the sacred connections to eros and power disappear and with them the living import of community. Thus, what has been called society (*Gesellschaft*) arises. Society, however, is only an unreal abstraction, a system of rational relationships of individuals having equal rights, without the import of community. But subjective naturalistic demonries break into this importless form.

In perfect society, free competition replaces the distribution of goods according to a hierarchy of intrinsic power. The liberal idea of free personality is distorted naturalistically and subjectively. The strongest intellectual and voluntaristic power has the greatest opportunities for victory in the rational process of utilizing things. The infinite drive to dominate things, supported by the subjective eros of every individual, leads to an endless conflict of all against all. Wherever communities are formed in this conflict, they are determined by their conflict against others; their goal is their common interest. And this holds not only for associations expressly created for this purpose, but it penetrates also into communities having other bases: family, class, sex, town, and nation become associations of economic interest, as far as the irrational powers that have brought them forth as communities allow. The autonomous and limitless economy begins its struggle for primacy over all other social functions and achieves it. In the degree to which it succeeds, however, it creates social situations that bear in themselves the unmistakable stamp of the demonic. As soon as the relationship of persons to each other has been subsumed in a relationship defined by pure justice, and as soon as the content of common work has become the economic utilization of things, the social power structure is determined exclusively by the economic power structure. This is conditioned, however, on the one hand, by traditional sacramental power positions that have lost their meaning, and, on the other, by personal qualities that correspond to the infinite rational utilization of things, qualities that are especially cultivated by a religious, theo-cratic spirit, for example, in Judaism and Calvinism. Upon these presuppositions arises the purely objective predominance of capital, which, on the one hand, formally gives every individual his due, but, on the other, integrates every individual into the system of the rational economic process, in which there are only objective de-pendent relations but no intrinsic eros and power relationships. This system of purely objective power, on the one hand, and of purely objective dependence, on the other, led to the class struggle peculiar to the capitalist era. Class struggle is not a universal social phenomenon but the consequence of a rationally formed economic social order in which intrinsic power relations have become extrinsic. The predominance of capital leads necessarily to class struggle, because a purely subjective will founded on eros and power takes the rational economic instrument into its service. But, at the same time, the rational character of the capitalist economy impedes this conflict to an extraordinary degree because there are only a few who have the rational qualities to manage the economy.

It follows from this that religious socialism must affirm the class struggle, not absolutely but according to the conditions of historical reality. The class struggle is a defense against an injustice that has brought about the radical pursuit of human rights—a pursuit that has no intrinsic import. The class struggle is itself, however, exactly like competition, an expression of the demonic character of capitalist economy. The intrinsic limits of the class struggle are such that it must remain in the sphere of the infinite rational will of the in-dustrial economy. But in this sphere, the objectification of power relations is inevitable. The bearers of power, supported by the sub-jective will to power and equipped with superior rational and eco-nomic power, break every heteronomous bond. For them there can be no other will, because there is no other import for them. Likewise, the oppressed are necessarily mechanized, since it is only in this mechanization that they can be used for the common goal. There-fore, religious socialism must establish a goal for the class struggle which will put it beyond the limits of the rational economic will. Its ultimate goal must be precisely liberation from the ethos of the limitless rational economy and the realization of a theonomous economic attitude. The problem of the predominance of capital cannot be solved on its own basis, so long as the demonry of the infinite will of a subjective economy prevails. To suppose that the predominance of capital would be broken by the socialization of the means of production is to overlook the fact that the subjective will of eros and power has supported the rational economy and that the latter must break down as soon as this support is eliminated without a substitute. Socialization can succeed only when a community can give to a common economy a meaning that replaces the subjective will to power with a universal religious eros. Only such an economic meaning rooted in the Unconditional can make leaders into bearers of intrinsic power, can demechanize those who are led, and can give to them the consciousness of participation in a common creativity. Theonomous power and gradations of power and meaning must replace rational power relations. Because it is taken up into the universal eros, subjective eros loses its harshness.

The concept of socialization thereby also acquires a new meaning. Socialization in the sense of state socialism is a counterconcept that is without eros and is opposed to the subjectivity of absolute private property. Whereas absolute private property is a consequence of the isolated formal personality, legally defined, state socialism is a consequence of the formal rationalized constitutional state *(Rechts-staat)*. Where, on the contrary, social relations are determined by the intrinsic power and erotic energy of the individual and of communities that posit justice, there appears, in spite of the full recognition of the personality formally equal before the law, the idea of the fief, that is, the idea of a possession or disposition *(Verfügung)* of goods according to the intrinsic power and significance of the individual and of the particular community for the life import of the whole. Naturally, this right of possession is discontinued when the individual and the community no longer have significance for the whole. Therefore, possession loses its exclusiveness; it becomes representative and makes possible an inner participation of all in the fief over which the individual has jurisdiction. Therefore, religious socialism cannot advocate the erosless expropriation of property any more than it can advocate the subjective dynamic right of possession or disposition. It looks to the realization of the theonomous demand through the right of possession built upon the fief idea and upon representative property.

4. The bearer of all justice is the community that posits justice, namely, the state. What community it is that posits justice is a matter of indifference. At the present time, nations are the essential bearers of the political idea. In the sacramental spiritual situation the state is borne by the stratum that carries within itself the import of the whole in the most powerful way. It has authority; for all authority is founded cultically and sacramentally. With the sacramental quality of authority is connected, however, the demonic oppression of those subject to the law as well as of those outside it. Consequently, the theocratic reaction necessarily has democratic and universalistic tendencies. A perfect theocracy would realize democracy within a state and a unified system of international justice. This is the ideal of radical political democracy which, disregarding all irrational powers, recognizes only rational individuals and rational universality. The fulfillment of the democratic ideal would mean the dissolution of the political into a universal self-sufficient organism of justice, that is, pure practical form.

But justice needs for its realization a will that posits and upholds it. In every moment, formlessness and arbitrariness contradict pure form. Justice needs power in order to be realized—power that in the struggle with arbitrariness becomes force. Social eros, which gives to justice an individual creative content, unites itself with power, which is inherent in every situation where justice is posited. However, as soon as radical democracy has driven out sacramental import, both justice and eros, indissolubly joined to the essence of the state, are distorted into the naturalistically demonic. There are essentially two powers that struggle for the state, economic power and national power. Over against them stand what remains of the old cultic aristocracies or hierarchies, on the one hand, and democracy and the national bureaucracy representing political form, on the other. The formation of parties in contemporary Germany arises out of this situation. From the point of view of the individual, democracy represents the rational idea of form, as does the bureaucracy from a universal point of view. The former is strongly sustained by powers of the liberal economy, the latter is supported by elements of the old sacramental authorities. Beside these are the old conservatives as pure representatives of the formerly cultic aristocracy that has since become naturalistic in many ways. The Center is supported by hierarchically heteronomous powers, an after-effect of a former theonomy. Finally, there are the Liberal party and its counterpart, the communist-socialistic reaction, and the nationalistic movement, which is united with industry in the national-liberal idea, and with the conservative aristocracy in the German national idea. The demonic character of economic predominance is revealed in the utilization of the rational form of political justice to establish the predominance of capital, partly through purely economic power, and partly through a politically active superior force based upon the latter. It is also revealed in the previously mentioned effects of this predominance in social life. The demonic character of nationalism is manifest in the relations of the states to each other, in the suspension of justice toward a foreign nation, and in the domestic political and social repercussions of this breakdown of the idea of justice.

The idea of nationhood in the sense of the present nation state is not a direct consequence of an original sacramental national consciousness. It is, rather, sustained by the Jewish-Christian repudiation of national divinities and by medieval theonomy. The contemporary nation arose with the dissolution of medieval supranational theonomy. Modern nationalism was born as a theocratic imperialism. All the great European nation-states are imperialistic, not because of a primitive naturalistic will to power; rather, they are imperialistic as bearers of theocratic ideas. This is especially the case with that nation which is religiously most theocratic, England. Only with the disappearance of the theocratically religious spirit did the subjective national will, founded on eros and power, seize the theocratic-rational form of the state and create nationalism as a religious demonry. Nationalism and economic will are opposed to each other in many ways. Their demonry is revealed in the most pernicious form as soon as they are united, as, for example, in the [First] World War.

The following basic guidelines (*Grundlinien*) emerge out of this situation for religious socialism. In domestic politics, commitment to a political party is out of the question. Religious socialism must struggle against the remains of the sacramental—that is, hierarchic and aristocratic—forms of power that contradict the affirmation of pure justice. At the same time, it must combat the rise of naturalistic forms of power, of industrialism, of nationalism, or every other emerging will to power that takes the rational form of the state into its service. It must affirm, as a universal form, the thoroughly rationalized democratic constitutional state. But this form, which is only abstract and regulative and never a reality, must be filled with the sacred import of a creative theonomy. The state must be supported by eros and by the intrinsic power of those in whom theonomous import is most powerfully revealed. It must carry within itself a living system of tensions in which the economic idea, the national idea, race (*Bluthaft*), etc., are evaluated according to their significance for the absolute all-embracing idea. Formal equality must be embraced and fulfilled to the breaking point. It must be fulfilled, not by a naturalistic demonic inequality but, rather, by a sacred divine inequality, an inequality that is founded upon the tension of theonomous power and erotic drive. Precisely because of this tension, this inequality is one with a freedom that does not mean the right of subjective arbitrariness but, rather, the possibility of an essential development.

By way of analogy, the same thing holds for foreign policy. Religious socialism must combat the demonry of naturalistic nationalism, especially when it seeks to give itself sacramental consecration. It must also affirm the all-embracing theocratic idea of justice—justice that is not an empty form negating power and eros and therefore subject to exploitation by an arbitrary national will but, rather, justice as a structure of national and racial powers. Just as the strongest bearers of theonomy within a political realm should comprise the leading class of a nation, so the strongest bearers of the theonomous idea of humanity should constitute the leadership of nations. Not education in itself, not blood in itself, not rational power in itself, not culture in itself, not even subjective originality or genius will create the inherently powerful theonomous leading class, only the fullness of the power of sacred import that supports the whole. Only when subjective eros and subjective power have entered into sacred eros and sacred power do they create an inwardly qualified and therefore firmly established leading class.

This point of view brings religious socialism into opposition with a pacifism that radically negates justice, domestic and foreign.

Views such as those of Tolstoi only appear to have something to do with religious socialism. In fact, they nullify it, inasmuch as they do not recognize one of its basic principles, namely, the affirmation of the form of justice. They fail to see that justice can assert itself as justice only by restraint (*Zwang*) of arbitrary will, and that the elimination of restraint would give power to arbitrary will—thus it would mean a surrender of the theocratic to the demonic. Or, on the other hand, they proclaim a utopian faith in a world without arbitrariness, incapable of the demonic, but also, therefore, a world without eros and power, and hence an uncreative world. They proclaim a mystical dissolution of form. Religious socialism rejects mystical as well as naturalistic anarchism. It insists upon the form of justice and, accordingly, affirms the force that maintains it. This applies not only to domestic but also to foreign policy. Just as the naturalistic anarchism of war is to be rejected, so also is the mystical anarchism of religious pacifism, which does not oppose the lawbreaker or which in a utopian manner denies individual creative powers that are rich with tension. There is no direct way from the mystical idea of community to the creation of political form. Between the two stands justice, and the justice-bearing power, and the use of force against injustice. Only the saint and the holy community can renounce justice in a symbolically representative sense, but the recognition of justice and its stability presupposes that their renunciation of justice is meant to have religious and not anarchistic meaning. The state, however, can never renounce the community that bears justice or the force that maintains it.

5. The state as the community that maintains justice is the most comprehensive social phenomenon. At the same time it provides the rational framework for all others. But social life is not the same as its political form (*staatlichrechtliches Form*). There is an autonomous social form not bound by formal justice, a form that is represented symbolically in custom, tradition, tact, etc. On account of their stronger opposition to the rationalizing of justice, these forms have been bearers of import longer than things that have been legally defined. Consequently, they have also been endowed for a longer time with a cultic-sacramental quality, and they have been emptied less than the others. But the difference is only relative. On the one hand, rational justice seeks to absorb into itself as extensively

as possible the immediate and symbolic forms of community, and, on the other hand, the rise of autonomous personality leads to a disintegration of the immediate social forms. The theocratic reaction against the demonic suppression of personality gives rise to this development, as, for example, in relations between the sexes, in family relationships, in associations based on generation and status, in the relationship to authority, etc. Here, theocracy signifies everywhere the liberation of autonomous personality, the dissolution of sacramental consecration, and a demand for free formation of community. Religious import, which is vital in theocracy, becomes operative in the inner life of the personality and gives rise to the sphere of religious and psychic intimacy so characteristic of Calvinist theocracy. The communities, above all the state, are wholly deprived of their import. Only in the family does there remain a residue of sacramental immediacy. But it is always more and more limited by the intrusion of economic egoism in the family. The free communities that served to advance the theocratic idea become administrative associations in the service of the subjective will of eros and power. Moreover, personality is deprived of its holy import the more it becomes autonomous and rational. It becomes the bearer of pure reason, an abstraction whose sublime character should not conceal its unreality or its fate, namely, that the form of pure reason is seized, filled, and broken through by the powers of subjective eros. They become bourgeois ethics and a prey to economic will to power. The mechanism of economic necessity takes the place of the abstract order of duty; the dictates of an economic leader take the place of the law of reason. The import of the community vanishes and the forms of community become symbols of a community of interest under whose cover the conflict of interests and subjective eros make sport.

It becomes the task of religious socialism to combat sacramental demonries in all social relations, for example, sacramental pride and honor that destroy personality, and to sustain the form of autonomous personality and of free community. At the same time, however, it must combat the demonries that invade pure forms, and the arbitrariness of subjective eroticism and of subjective will-to-power. It is important that religious socialism strive for a theonomous community in which social forms, morals, and traditions do not simultaneously express and conceal the economic power-struggle and subjective eroticism but, rather, symbolize a holy import that penetrates the eros and power relations of a rich social life, and which secures them and subjects them to an unconditional idea. Only a "metaphysical" community can support and fulfill communities. All others end finally in arbitrariness and interest, in chance and mechanization.

The spiritual or cultural community (*Gemeinschaft in Geist und Kultur*) cannot restore the lost import of community. For spirit, which is mere form without the import of the conditioned, dissolves the community. The autonomous form of culture, formal education, is available to only a few; it isolates; it is subjectively conditioned; it drives toward ceaseless opposition of all against all. It creates a small educated class and leaves to everyone else the worn-out and corrupt forms, the *kitsch* in art and science, in morals and jurisprudence (*Rechtsauffassung*). The result is that an exclusive, educated aristocracy takes the place of a representative aristocracy of the spirit. Even the spirit that is filled with the import that supports the whole is, as spirit and as formative power (*Formung*), accessible only to the few. But it creates symbols that can be understood by all. In contrast, education, having appropriated form without content, remains unintelligible, encourages false imitation, and makes the gulf separating economic classes unbridgeable. The demonic force of inferior value among the masses is one of the most disastrous effects of exclusive formal education. Instinct lays hold of form and misshapes it into its own. But the subjective eroticism that belongs in the spiritual realm to the bearers of education contradicts the essence of spirit in the same way, and has the same demonically destructive effect as the deformation of the spirit among the masses. Only a theonomous spirituality produces an aristocracy of spirit. For by means of a metaphysical intention shared by all, every theonomous form becomes a common symbol that does not separate but unites.

Here also the guiding principles of religious socialism are clear: to recognize autonomous education in opposition to hierarchical or aristocratic heteronomies, to combat the subjective eros of the bearers of education and of the mechanization of the spirit among the masses, to strive for an import that creates common, theoretical and practical, formative symbols that are maintained by a representative spiritual aristocracy that lives by the same import as do all others.

Thus, in the theoretical as well as in the practical sphere, the basic guidelines (*Grundlinien*) of what religious socialism has to struggle against and what it has to strive for have been drawn. It must combat the demonic in the naturalistic as well as in the sacramental sense, and it must strive for theonomy in the sense of the unity of form and import. These are its tasks: the conquest of sacramental demonry through a theocratic struggle, and the pursuit of autonomous form, but not in order to come to a halt when it reaches autonomous form, for that is not possible—autonomous form is emptied of divine import, and forthwith it is a prey to demonic import—but in order to permit autonomous form to be filled with theonomous import. Its opponent is the demonic. But this does not mean that the irrational forces, that is, power and eros, which support the demonic must be annihilated; the attempt to do this is either rational utopianism or the mystical destruction of form. On the contrary, the same element that is destructive in the demonic (because it is manifestly destructive of form) will come to be seen as the divine, that is, as form-fulfilling, in theonomy. This corresponds to the idea of Kairos, which also does not lead to rational utopianism or to the mystical negation of the world but, rather, to a new and creative fulfillment of forms with an import borne by power and eros but penetrated by obedience to unconditioned form. It is therefore not demonic but divine.

The different aspects of the theonomous idea have only been suggested in what has been said. They have not been fully worked out. This is the task of religious socialism, theoretical and practical. The decisive element, however, the new breakthrough of import, is not a matter of work. Rather, it is fate and grace. Belief in the Kairos is the expression of the consciousness of existing in that fate and of being touched by a new breakthrough of the Unconditional. All rational work in theory and practice can have no other meaning than to give expression to this import in every sphere of life.

4. THE WAY OF RELIGIOUS SOCIALISM

The consciousness of Kairos in the sense of an emerging theonomy creates a community of those who are filled with the same import and who strive for the same goal. It is a community of those who hear the call of the Kairos and understand themselves in it. Such a community is not a church in the sacramental spiritual sense, for it does not proceed from fixed sacred forms and symbols. Rather, it stands in theocratic and autonomous criticism before the given symbols whose demonic distortion it fights. This applies to all existing confessions but not to all in the same way. Religious socialism stands nearest to that confession that bears within itself the critical-theocratic element most strongly, although it knows that it is nearer in terms of goal to those confessions in which the theonomous idea has found expression, though a demonically degenerate one. This determines its peculiar double attitude toward the Reformed and the Catholic expressions of the Christian idea. Thus, in its critical attitude it must go along with the radical forms of the Reformation, and in the theonomous idea it must go along with a Catholicism set free from demonic heteronomy. Moreover, it follows from this that religious socialism cannot be identified directly with any of the confessions. Still less is the community of those supported by the Kairos a separate confession, a religious sect. The formation of new religious communities does not proceed from autonomy and criticism but only from a new apprehension and transformation of old symbols. New religious creations stand in living connection with the creations of the past. They burst forth only out of the deepest tensions within a confession. Religious socialism, however, is born on the soil of critical autonomy. It has in itself no power to create symbols and it can therefore form no religious community in a special concrete sense. Whether in coming developments it will join in the formation of a religious community is a question that at present is without significance.

Religious socialism is no more identical with a cultural movement or a political party than it is with a religious confession. Religious socialism is therefore not identical with political socialism, nor does it form a party alongside it. It calls itself "socialism" because it has adopted the antidemonic socialist criticism historically and substantially and because it supports the political struggle of socialism as far as it intends to break the domination of political and social demonries. But religious socialism does not overlook the extent to which political socialism itself is possessed by these demonries, and, above all, it knows that the socialist idea should not be equated with the goal of political strategy. It must therefore repudiate giving religious consecration to a party as such or to an economic program as such. It keeps its eye open for the theonomous elements in other parties and movements as well. It cannot make fellowship with itself depend positively or negatively upon membership in a party. But it certainly calls for the recognition of the socialist criticism of culture and of the socialist struggle against sacramental and naturalistic demonries.

Religious socialism is a community of those who understand themselves in the consciousness of the Kairos and who struggle for the fate, that is, the grace, of theonomy. They can work in every party, confession, movement, so far as the latter make room for their work and allow for the struggle against the demonic elements within themselves. Only in this way can religious socialism protect itself from premature objectification, from becoming heteronomous, and thus from becoming subject to its own criticism. Certainly there can be more or less close alliances of those conscious of the Kairos. But they must retain a provisional character until symbols and forms are found that are the immediate expression of the total spiritual situation and which, therefore, do not operate rationally and heteronomously. The overcoming of the provisional, however, and the development of a new theonomy can occur only through a new creative breakthrough of the import that has been revealed in the symbols of the past. Without such a breakthrough a theonomous spiritual situation is impossible. However, when it has happened— and it is the Kairos faith that it is happening—then it pours forth into the forms that have been created out of its spirit, forms that religious socialism must help to create.

Christianity and Marxism*

It would make little sense to talk about Christianity and *Stalinism*, for the "and" would, after all, mean that the two relate not only negatively but also positively. This is not the case, though. Christianity affirms and Stalinism negates the value and dignity of personhood. From this difference follow mutually exclusive contrasts in all realms of life. There is the contrast between the Christian affirmation and the Stalinist negation of fairness in judges and the veracity of witnesses. There is the contrast between the Christian desire to heal every individual in his innermost being, and the Stalinist readiness to destroy the personal center of every individual through terror, to convert him into a thing. There is the contrast between the Christian affirmation of freedom as prerequisite to all spiritual creativity, and the Stalinist collectivization of the spirit and its bondage to predetermined models.

I could continue, but my theme is, after all, not "Christianity and Stalinism" but "Christianity and Marxism," and the difference between Marxism and Stalinism is the next matter of concern. Stalinism is the oriental totalitarian form of the Marxist movement, or more precisely, its radical reshaping under the conditions of the Russian-Asian tradition. Reshaping is not removal, and it is clear that even within Stalinism motifs of original Marxism are still operative. Yet the difference is fundamental. In order to understand it one must not only distinguish Stalinism from Marxism, but one must also consider the development that pre-Stalinist Marxism un-

* Translated by Charles W. Fox.

derwent, in Marx himself and in the Marxist movement. One can then distinguish several stages of development: first and foremost, the early writings of Marx; then his later work and the influence of Engels upon it; further, the development and internal tensions of German Social Democracy and German and Russian communism up to the time of Lenin. All this is Marxism, and each of these phases is important for a comparison of Christianity and Marxism. It is, however, my intention to limit my investigation to *one* phase, namely, the first. This requires no justification, for that is the phase neglected and often intentionally held in the dark by Marxist dogmaticians. Yet in that phase as nowhere else those themes become visible which were decisive for Marx himself and the masses of his followers, and without which his remarkable historical effect must remain unintelligible.

There are two fundamental motifs decisive in Marx's early development: his conception of man and his conception of history, and both display clear analogies with the Christian interpretation of man and history. At the same time, however, these notions exhibit that contrast with Christianity which has led to those developments in Marxism and Stalinism that have caused the analogy virtually to disappear.

That conception of man by Marx which comes to expression not only in his early writings, but stands behind all his work, even the latest, is most succinctly formulated in the notion of the alienation of man from himself, of dehumanization. Man is not in fact what he is essentially, and therefore could and should be; he has become estranged from his own essential nature. True humanity is impossible under the conditions of the early capitalistic social order. That holds especially for the proletariat, in whose existence alienation and dehumanization have progressed the furthest. But it applies also to the ruling classes, who can conceal the questionableness of their existence through wealth and culture and who create ideologies in order to justify exploitation of the other classes. Estrangement, according to Marx, is the fate of all groups in industrial society. True humanity is effective only in the form of a protest against estrangement, and since it is by the proletariat that this protest is most powerfully set forth, that group has a dual role: it is the locus of the deepest estrangement and at the same time the protest of true

humanity against that estrangement. The proletariat is both the re-
deemer and the one most in need of redemption.

The inner contradiction of this position had far-reaching consequences. It led in part to an unrealistic glorification of the proletariat, and in part to a realistic, but also risky, separation of the
proletariat into the masses and the avant-garde. To the avant-garde
could belong even nonproletarians, such as Marx himself. And these
individuals became the nucleus of the bureaucracy that, after the
successful revolution in Russia, subjugated to itself the proletariat,
and through them the entire populace. This is one of the lines that
leads from Marx to Stalinism. So we find in Marx these basic ideas:
first of all, man as he is essentially, then man alienated and dehumanized through capitalism, then man rebelling against his dehumanization, and finally the man of the coming classless society
who is again what man essentially is and should be. All this is embraced in the concept of estrangement derived from Hegel and
originating in the prophetic-Christian tradition.

It is not difficult to see the analogies and contrasts of the Christian
view of man to that of the Marxist. What Marx calls alienation is in
Christian conceptualization the fall of man from his essential innocence into a situation of conflict with himself and his creative
ground. Man is not what he could and should be. That holds for the
individual as well as for society; and it is also true of the universe,
which participates in the fate of man. Man stands against man,
group against group, being against being. Schism characterizes everything that exists in the soul of the individual, in humanity, and in
the universe.

The contrast with the Marxist view of man, however, is clear in
spite of all these analogies. The "fall" in Christian conception is
universal; "estrangement" in the Marxist view is bound to a special
period of time. The Christian symbol of paradise is transhistorical;
the Marxist symbol of primitive communism, historical. In Marxism
a historical group, the proletariat or the avant-garde, can overcome
estrangement; in Christianity every social group stands in need of
redemption and is incapable of delivering itself or other groups. The
power of redemption breaks into the historical process vertically and
is not its product. That has a decisive practical consequence. Christianity places every human group under judgment, from which in

Marxism the proletariat is exempted. Christianity knows of no exceptions; it accuses itself of creating ideologies; it constantly places itself under this suspicion.

The Marxist elite identifies itself with *the* truth, and thereby gains the good conscience to persecute and, if possible, destroy every opponent. Where Marxism has gained absolute power and retained its messianic claim, it has developed methods of terror whose aim is to subdue not only every real enemy but also every potential one. Even if Christianity has approached this position in many moments of its history, it has nevertheless developed reactions that have ever and again shattered totalitarian claims. But Stalinism, that is, the totalitarian form of Marxism, has never developed such reactions—and this is due in part to the fact that the Marxist doctrine of estrangement was not intended to apply universally to mankind, but was restricted to the situation within the capitalism of Marx's own time. Marx perceives a "historically reparable" alienation where Christianity sees a "transhistorical" fall that can be healed only transhistorically through the appearance of the Messiah, who may be identified with neither the proletariat nor any other human group.

As is customary in Marx and in Marxism, the interpretation of man determines the interpretation of history. It is characteristic of Marx's conception of history that he seeks to understand nature from the point of view of history and not history from the point of view of nature. Marx's interpretation of history is historical rather than naturalistic. His emphasis upon the historicity of man is so strong that he derives the character of what is "nature" for man from his historical situation. He knows no nature in itself, only a history in itself, namely, the history of human production through which man has made himself into that which he is. Thus Marx is a long way from the circular theory of history of the Greeks, with its doctrine of the recurrence of the same events. He is closer to the Jewish prophetic-apocalyptic conception of history. For him history is a unique process with a unique goal. The beginning of the world-historical processes is what Marx in occasional remarks calls the transition from primitive communism to the class society. This transition is a presupposition, not a determinable event. History as we know it is a history of class struggles, a history Marx also called, in a well-known statement, "prehistory." It leads to the classless society with which the true history of mankind begins. It would perhaps have been more precise if Marx had called this third period that of the uninterrupted development of man in his "reunited essence." The alienation of the second period is overcome. The division of classes, with its fateful effects not only upon the social but also upon the psychic existence of man, is eliminated.

But all this lies in the future, and one can say nothing concrete about it. How man will appear when united with his essential nature cannot be known in the state of estrangement. One knows only that he will possess the opposite of that character which under the conditions of class society drives him into conflict with himself and with other human beings and groups. Marx has painted neither a past nor a future paradise but, rather, history so far as it is an object of experience stretched across the frame of three periods. Thus the first and third periods serve more as directional lines for the understanding of the second period than as concretely described realities. On the other hand, the analysis of the present is decisive, for in the present the enormous tension between the end of the second period and the expected beginning of the third period is experienced. This tension has given victorious buoyancy to many earlier revolutions, as also to the revolutionary movements incited by Marx.

The analogies between these ideas and the prophetic-primitive Christian preaching are quite evident. The Christian symbols of paradise, of human history burdened with a curse, of the fullness of time in which the kingdom of heaven has drawn nigh, and of the new earth upon which the kingdom of God is erected—all of this evidences an interpretation of history that is similar to the Marxist one, and indeed, historically considered, more original. In the New Testament period it generated the same enormous tension and victorious ardor as Marxism has done. And yet as was the case in the relation of the Christian and Marxist conception of man, so also here, the analogy has more and more been swallowed by the contrast. In Marxism the three periods of world history are conceived linearly. All three periods lie on a horizontal plane in space and time. By contrast the Christian interpretation may be compared to an even curve that emerges from and returns again into the transhistorical. Prophecy knows of that vertical dimension which Marxism has repudiated as ideology, and this contrast has profound practical consequences. Whenever the third period, the age of fulfillment, is awaited within history, the actuality of history disappoints every such expectation and exposes it as utopian. Psychologically and politically, that can have two opposite effects: either a deep disappointment is evoked, and with it an often cynical alienation from every historical expectation, *or* the determination is born to hold fast to one's expectations with every means available. When this latter happens, a period of reorganization is established, and all the methods of totalitarian domination are employed to defend this period, namely, the time after the victorious revolution, against criticism and transition to something new. The strongest weapon of this defense against presumed change is terror. That is a second line that leads from Marxism to Stalinism.

Christianity awaits a consummation of history which emerges out of the vertical dimension, beneath whose judgment every historical epoch stands. This excludes utopianism, disappointment, and terror, and creates an attitude in which one always looks upward at the same time that one looks forward. That raises the question concerning the powers that determine the historical process. One customarily sums up the Marxist answer in the concept of "dialectical materialism." That is possible, but it is accurate only if the two ambiguous words, "materialism" and "dialectical," are understood in the Marxist sense and are unambiguously defined. For Marx materialism means the dependence of every aspect of the historical process upon the manner in which man reproduces his existence. That happens basically through economic production, which therefore is decisive for the whole development of history.

This definition shows that Marxist materialism is not metaphysical materialism. In his *Theses against Feuerbach,* Marx expressly opposed metaphysical materialism. Otherwise it would not have been possible for him to call his materialism "dialectical." It is one of the tragedies of Western cultural history that the dialectical method, by means of which most leading philosophers from the time of Plato to Hegel have worked, has in part degenerated into a political slogan, and has in part been equated with supposedly inextricable social mechanisms. But dialectic was not a clanking mechanism for Marx;

it was a method of describing social powers, conflicts, and tendencies. Like Hegel, though, he was aware that without the passion of human activity nothing can be realized in history—and hence his passionately expressed appeals to the proletariat and his equally passionate declaration of war on the bourgeoisie. Both are meaningless if history is an automatic process, and dialectic the theoretical description of inextricable mechanisms.

Whenever Marxism and Christianity are compared, it is often the idea of dialectical materialism in which people believe they see the contrast most clearly. But that is only partially correct. Something of the realism of the Christian interpretation of man is to be found in historical materialism, and in the idea of historical dialectic there is something of the Christian notion of providence. And in both ideas one finds expressed that indissoluble interweaving of freedom and fate which is characteristic of the Christian as well as the Marxist view of the world. Both lose their depth as soon as the unity of freedom and fate is broken: freedom becomes political caprice and fate a mechanical necessity.

The analogy between Christianity and Marxism holds up to this point, even in the question of dialectical materialism, but it extends no further. Rather, as in the other points, it has more and more been swallowed by the contrast. The decisive opposition between dialectical materialism and the Christian belief in providence is neither the dialectical nor the materialistic element, but the contrast between purely inner-historical factors that, according to Marx, determine history, and that combination of inner- and supra-historical factors which, in Christian idea, control history. It is the complete absence of the transhistorical element in Marxism which not only brings it into opposition to Christianity, but in Stalinism even drives it towards consequences that contradict its original impulses. It is not, however, the intellectual contrast between Christianity and Marxism which is finally decisive, but the practical one: the realization of two possibilities of life. Christianity views the human situation, including human history, from a stance between time and eternity. It perceives the infinite dignity of the individual person which follows from his relation to eternity. It perceives the boundary of everything human in space and time under the conditions of finitude and guilt. And it poses the question concerning a reconciliation in which the temporal is elevated into the eternal and the eternal becomes effective in the realm of time. Marxism perceives the human situation, including human history, as completely bound to time. It can therefore only work towards an organization of society within time; and it must, so far as it is convinced of the truth of its own conception, try to realize it by every means, even such as those in which human dignity is disregarded. It awaits a reconciliation that occurs in space and time, and it is therefore open to utopianism, and to the disappointment that follows upon every utopia, and ultimately to terror. The decision between these two life possibilities is neither economic nor political; it is religious.

The State as Expectation and Demand*

1. EXPECTATION AND DEMAND

There are two polar possibilities for a contemporary as opposed to a historical or systematic discussion of the state. One possibility is to demand a state in which the ideal of the state has been fulfilled. The other possibility is to reflect upon the state that can be hoped for on the basis of its present reality. The first way, when consistently worked out, is utopian. The second, with certain qualifications, is dialectical. Utopianism looks to the ideal, and opposes it to reality as a demand upon it or as a goal to be worked out within it. Dialectic looks to reality and to the trends inherent in it, and places itself in the service of these trends. The conflict of Marxism against the older socialist groups was a conflict of dialectic against the utopian idea, of the reckoning of reality against the intuition of the ideal.

Nevertheless, there can be no pure antithesis between the two attitudes. Utopianism cannot form its ideal without also being influenced by the actual situation, whether it is aware of it or not. But the more it is aware of it, the more it approaches the dialectical conception. On the other hand, dialectical reckoning of the trends dominant in reality is not possible without the cooperation of the ideal form, which can affect it consciously or unconsciously. The

* Translated by Victor Nuovo.

more it is raised to consciousness, the more the dialectical attitude approaches the utopian. It is true that Marxism was a conflict of the dialectical against the utopian idea, but the utopian element was taken up into the Marxist dialectic. It is also true that Marxism was a party, but at the same time it stood above parties.

There is, therefore, an attitude in which the utopian idea and dialectic are united, one that is at the same time demand and expectation. But it is not as if demand in some aspects were united with expectation in some other aspects. Rather, together they form a unity. Reckoning of what is to come must not be a casual consideration. Rather, it must be a responsible and co-creative intuition. Also, the positing of the ideal must not be an abstract construction. Rather, born in the present, it must push forth beyond the present. Responsible intuition must be the unity of dialectic and the utopian idea. It is the methodological ideal for a consideration of realities like the state as they exist in the present. And for the sake of this methodological ideal, expectation and demand are combined in a common theme.

Responsible intuition is born of the present. But the present is an ambiguous concept. It all depends upon the depths in which the present is contemplated. The actuality of the present lies at different levels of depth. So-called *Realpolitik* seeks the present at a very shallow level, in the sphere of opportunism which is born of the moment but not of the present. Responsibility at this level is a responsibility in the purely intellectual region of the soul. But it is not a responsibility that reaches the ultimate level of being. Accordingly, here the unity of responsibility and demand is without tension and without power. The present must be more than the momentary. Acting and knowing out of the present must be more than real-political action and impressionistic knowledge. The depth of the present is that point in it in which something unconditional, a source of meaning, invades it and leads it beyond itself and its contingencies. The responsible intuition of the state occurs where the state is seen from the viewpoint of a meaning-giving principle that gives to the contemporary state its depth and its limit. Only in such an intuition is expectation and demand united full of power and tension.

2. THE STATE

The state is a community tempered by justice. There are two parts to this definition. In the first instance, the state exists where justice is posited. The state is the bearer of justice, and where justice is upheld, there is the state. For the formal definition of the concept it is of no importance whether the bearer of justice is the patriarchal family or a nation inhabiting a portion of the earth. The function, to bear justice, to posit it and to enforce it defines the essence of the state. But at the same time, the state requires a community that has the power of justice, power over itself which it reveals in positing its justice. Where there is no intrinsic power (*Selbstmächtigkeit*) there is no state. Where there is no power to posit and to enforce justice there is no state. In the development of the state, the power of a community obtains form, and thereby existence. The state is the power of a community that realizes itself in the positing of justice.

A definition of the political cannot fail to take into account the relation to justice and power. Indeed, it is not even possible to define justice without power or power without justice. Therefore, the view that accounts for the state in terms of the subjection of a class or race by a victorious oppressor is entirely inadequate. The union of conqueror and conquered in a state presupposes the fundamental subordination to one system of justice (*ein Recht*) which is binding for both parties. The system of justice can guarantee numerous privileges for the victorious party. But even privileges are obligations (*Bindungen*), and owe their existence to the system of justice by which they are guaranteed. Theories of power can, in certain historical cases, account for the rise of a certain form of the state. But whenever the rise of states is accounted for by conquest, the essential form of the state is already presupposed. This political form belongs to the essence of power itself, which is different from the actual overpowering of one by another, so that it is the expression of a real and therefore inherently recognized possession of power (*Mächtigkeit*) by an individual or a group. Inasmuch as this possession of power is revealed in justice, the relationship of justice to power is constitutive of its concept.

But the isolation of justice also negates the understanding of what constitutes the state. Justice that merely moves to and fro within itself in its universality is an illusion. A definite, concrete drive that is grounded in life reveals itself in justice. There is no abstract justice separated from such a vital foundation. It would have neither content nor the possibility of existence. It comes into existence only through the power that posits it and upholds it, and just from this power comes the concrete content that creates and expresses life. This fact is overlooked by all abstract democratic theories that want to separate justice from the basis of power on which it rests, and which make the state into a system of automatic justice without foundation in life (*eine vital unfundierten Rechtsmaschine*). They all fail to see that the positing of justice and its enforcement finally rests on a decision, and that in every system of political justice (*Staatsrecht*), even the democratic, there is a legal procedure for decision (*eine Entscheidung gebende Instanz*) which, in itself, no longer stands under justice, even though it is empowered by justice for its decision. In this legal process the justice-bearing power of the community is revealed. But this means that if validation belongs to the essence of justice, power, which is posited in validation, belongs to it. Even from this point of view, justice and power belong indissolubly together in the sphere of the political. On the basis of this universal definition it is necessary to inquire first into the content and then into the form of the state. The content of political life is determined, on the one hand, by spiritual (*geistige*) life, and, on the other hand, by economic life, whereas the form of the state is represented on the one hand by its internal structure and on the other hand, outwardly, by its boundaries.

3. STATE AND SPIRIT

The relation of the state to spiritual values (*den geistigen Werten*) is decisively revealed in the state's relation to public cultus and to public education. Modern theories of the state can be classified under three symbols according to their definition of this relationship. Hobbes has given the first symbol in his *Leviathan*. It is a demonic symbol, and signifies the all-consuming might of the state. All spiritual values are subjected to it, and are permitted or excluded by it.

It determines the public cultus. It determines what shall be taught, and what artists shall create. It passes judgment on private life as far as its structure is concerned. Only pure inwardness remains free. But this inwardness may not assume outward expression beyond what corresponds to the interest of the state, where it may result in a total contradiction between what the individual intends and what he as a citizen is obliged publicly to do. Whereas Hobbes calls the state a "mortal God," one must, rather, say that it resembles a demon who does not want to die.

The other symbol is, as Hegel saw it, the state as God on earth. It is, in contrast to the demonic, a divine symbol. It receives its divinity, not from its all-consuming might, but from its character as bearer of all spiritual values. It does not dictate from outside what is permitted in public life as forms of spirit, of cultus, and of life. Rather, it is itself the realization of the spirit in history. Art, science, morality, and religion are actual in it. It does not merely allow their existence, it is [identical with] them. The meaning of history, the realization of the world spirit in the spirits of nations arises in it and is manifest through it. Therefore, it is the "earthly God." All holiness is concentrated in it.

The third symbol is the "Watchman State" as it prevailed in liberalism as a reaction against the oppression of princely protection in all matters of the spirit and of life. An extremely profane or secular symbol takes the place of the demonic and the divine symbols. The state has no consecration. Spiritual matters, religion and the fashioning of life, develop freely, protected by the state in their external existence. The state has a purely negative function. It struggles against the powers of the night which threaten the peaceful process of life. No divine consecration is necessary for this, and no wealth of demonic power, only just enough power to protect justice. All inherent power belongs to society which is protected by it. Society, the individuals in it, and their free associations, are the bearers of art and science, of religion and the moral life, of cultus and education. The object of political theory is, as Humboldt attempted in an early work, "to define the limits of the state."

From the perspective of each of these three symbols of the state, the demonic, the divine, and the secular, let us now approach the present [situation], first outside Germany. Here only a general outline of the situation can be presented. Thus, in Anglo-American countries, society is the bearer of spiritual values, of the cultus and of education. Only the Anglican Church, remaining from feudal times, is an exception. But since it is an exception, it is not of any decisive significance for the English conception of the state. That the English Parliament can decide about details of the Anglican prayer book is of no consequence for the idea of the state itself. Nevertheless, the English state cannot be comprehended simply by means of the secular symbol. It is much more than a watchman state. It is the direct expression of English being, just as the American state is of American being. The characteristic unity of the national will to power and theocratic world expansion, which constitutes English and, with important variations, American being is realized in [the state] and is guided by it into existence. But at the same time, this unity is directly revealed in English spiritual and social life with its strong conservative tendencies. In state and in spirit, English being reveals itself in the same way. Therefore, the state can allow the spirit freedom. English society takes care that the spirit does not move against the state, nor the state against the spirit. Both are born of the same lineage. It is similar in America. In both countries, therefore, the problem of the relation of state and spirit is not a prominent one.

It is entirely different in those countries where there is a dictatorship, above all in Italy and Russia. Here there is no ruling society which can experience state and spirit in the same way as the expression of its essence. Here, rather, there is a ruling group whose spirit stands generally in contradiction to the spirit of those who are ruled. Here there is no other option but the compulsive internalization of this spirit, especially in the younger generation. Education originates exclusively from the state, that is, from the power group that rules the state. Nevertheless, even this state tries to give itself an explicit consecration, for the sake of the enthusiasm necessary to support a dictatorship. In Italy, for instance, Fascism is attempting to juxtapose an ancient pagan-state ideology with an alliance with the Papacy, an attempt, of course, which has little chance to endure. In Russia, the religious-eschatological ardor from the time of the revolution stands behind the state as a consecrating power and still permits the oppression of Greek Catholicism. But even if Bolshevism should attain complete neutrality, it would not be able to renounce the unexpressed religious consecration of its sovereignty, and, in that, it would never be entirely remote from the apocalyptic element in Russian piety. Even though, with such forms of dictatorship, the state cannot be classified as "God on earth"—in Russia it cannot just because the dissolution of the state belongs to the eschatological expectation of Marxism—nevertheless, the state exercises a surveillant force over the spirit which approaches the demonic.

In Germany, numerous remains of the medieval situation are found in which the churches are bearers of the formation of the spirit and of life, but as trustees and guardians of the state. Guardian, not only in the sense of "watchman," but also in the sense of granting privilege just to those forms which it supports, and discriminating against other groups. This relation still continues, often with amazing strength. Nevertheless, intrinsically, it has been discontinued, and doubtless because of the fact of the contradictions of confessions and world-views which is characteristic of the spiritual situation in Germany since the Reformation and the Enlightenment. It might now appear as if the English solution were adequate under these conditions. But this is not the case. A society that has been formed by a common spirit and life-style, and which bears state and spirit in the same way as its very own, is lacking. German society is radically divided and without a unified formation. The only unifying power is the state. Therefore, in Germany, the state cannot restrict itself by leaving spiritual life to society. It must counteract spiritual disintegration, which indeed also involves necessarily a disintegration in the understanding of the state and of justice. It must be more than an external guardian, but at the same time it must be less than a god or a demon. In this lies the extraordinary difficulty, but at the same time the unpleasant necessity, of a politics of culture on German soil. The attempt to create a way out through a neohumanistic pedagogy, or to demand an autonomous pedagogy, is no essential advance. For there is no autonomous pedagogy in the sense of independence from world-view and confession, and a new humanism could hardly serve as a unifying foundation of opposing tendencies. Neither could it impart to the Germans a unified spirit and life-form, nor a unified national consciousness of mission. The antitheses of Protestant and Catholic, proletarian and middle class, supranational and national, to name only the most important, are not dissolved in humanism. The situation of brokenness in Germany is not to be set aside. Neither can the state become a god-demon, nor merely a secular "functionary." Rather, it must recognize the situation of brokenness and give it depth, by which it can become the expression of the brokenness of the human situation generally.

First and above all, the state must remain conscious of this, so that it may never be the bearer of the ultimate and unconditional meaning of life. Life in the state, the devotion to it, even the sacrifice of life to it, can never be absolutely full of meaning. The state is not the sphere of life in which truth, love, and holiness as such are intended. These all transcend it, even though they cannot come into existence without it. But as they cannot come into existence without it, the state participates in the holiness of that which it helps into existence, and therefore it participates in truth and love and has its value through them. So that it may not take the place of the holy, the state opposes every element of hypocrisy that inevitably accompanies every alliance of political will to power and religious demand. It does so even when this alliance is subjectively honorable, as frequently in the war of the Calvinist countries against Germany. So that it may not be reduced to the status of a mere negative functionary, the state opposes emptying political life of spirituality and holiness, which would assume for its acts the dignity of the creator of authentic value, and which would deliver sovereignty to irresponsible powers—which, moreover, would force spiritual matters into private and deprive them of the weight of a public concern. In this double negation, the Protestant attitude of the state toward spirit and cultus is revealed. It is an attitude that, on the one hand, forces everything onto the plane of the secular over against the Unconditional and Transcendent, recognizing no direct holiness, either of church or of state. On the other hand, it is an attitude that does not permit anything profane to rest in its profanity, but shakes it and establishes it through the relationship to the holy.

One can designate this relationship concretely as a "tacit transfer" (*stillschweigende Übertragung*) of spiritual and cultic things by the state to the bearers who are inherently capable of supporting them. That group is inherently capable of being the bearer of the spirit which serves the spirit with a responsibility that is free and which has no form, or only a very indefinite sociological one. That social group is inherently capable of bearing the holy, which is united in purpose with the "*Gestalt* of grace," that is, the church. But both groups stand in a hidden or a public alliance in which the one or the other can predominate, thus, for example, in the Middle Ages the church, and, in the present, the spiritual group. Moreover, this polarity cannot be entirely dissolved, either in favor of the church or in favor of the spirit. For church without free spirituality leads to apathy and idolatry, and spirit without church leads to vacuity and disintegration. And it is just this polarity that makes distance from both of them into an obligation for the state, and forces it into a broken relationship to spirit and cultus. It transfers to the spiritual group the responsibility for the spirit and to the church the responsibility for the holy. It does this tacitly. This means, *the state* transfers, that is, it will not let either of them go. For its own sake it must not, because justice without spirit and holiness is force and arbitrary decision. Second, this means, the state *transfers*, that is, it does not itself execute either function. It recognizes the necessary freedom of spirituality and the inviolability of the holy. It knows that here it only serves them, and that it cannot create them by positing justice. In the third place, this means, the state transfers *tacitly*, that is, the transfer is not an explicit act of justice. Indeed it is immanent in the positing of justice, but it is not an explicit and independent act of justice. If it were, then at the same time it would require more than its due and would give away more than it can spare. The tacit act leaves the boundaries undefined from both sides, and puts the decision only in specific concrete laws. Thus [the state] cannot, for example, give up control of the schools, but it is also incapable of providing by itself the goal and the content of education. It must tacitly transfer this task. And this is true of the polarity of spirit and church, when at a time of inferior symbolic power in the church, dominance even in education falls to the spirit. An evangelical politics of education would have to make these principles its own, and to keep itself equally far from confessional claims to power and from the demand for an autonomous state education. It is Protestant to demand a tacit transfer according to the current creative power of the spiritual and ecclesiastical groups.

4. THE STATE AND THE ECONOMY

The attitude of the state toward economy is throughout analogous to the relation of the state to spirit. Both economy and spirit are the direct productive factors to which the state gives existence through power and justice. Mercantilist economic theory corresponds to the symbol of Leviathan, and it reverts to state socialism and to a certain form of planned economy. The liberal view, which includes free trade, corresponds to the watchman symbol, whereas the state as God on earth reduces economic life to the lowest grade of holiness and incorporates or subordinates its higher functions. Mercantilism turns the state into the subject of the economic system (*Wirtschaft-subjekt*). To be sure, it is a state which, as a separate reality, has been raised above the feudal hierarchies, and which leads an independent existence represented in the absolute princes and supported by a bureaucracy and a professional military. The bearers of the state are at the same time the princes of the economic process. Commercial life (as well as the life of the spirit and the cultus) is a department of the state administration. The dominion of subjective reason is revealed in this attitude.

Over against it stands the dominion of objective reason, that is, reason that rediscovers itself in the objective world which was posited by it as the natural harmony of conflicting interests. The liberal view, which begins with this presupposition, locates the productive power of the economy in the unlimited economic energy of individual traders and industrialists (*Wirtschaftenden*), which is released for the greatest development by the conflict of all against all. Here the state can only be a hindrance. It must not hamper and it must not demand. The rationality (*die Vernunft*) of the economic process is guaranteed apart from it by the harmony in which the true interest of all is allied to the real interest of every individual. Belief in this harmony makes the intervention of the state superfluous and harmful. It has nothing to do except to guard with its means of power the free development of the powers of economic productivity. This is so in principle, but not in reality. The autonomous economy uses the state in order to restrict its autonomy for the benefit of a limited power group, externally and also within.

A monopolistic tendency which is as far-reaching as possible is in conflict with the national economy through the means of power. Tariffs, colonial conquests, and imperialistic wars signify the enlistment of the state for the goals of a national economic group, through whose hegemony the free counterplay of powers is restricted. And the same applies within. The guarantee of capital monopoly, which was established formerly in part on the basis of the feudal distribution of property, represents the actual exclusion of most from free competition. The concept of absolute property and its legal consolidation turns the liberal idea into its contrary for by far the greatest number of people. Then, on this ground, social demands are raised, whose fulfillment permanently restricts the autonomy of the economy from below, just as it is restricted from above by capital monopoly. Every socio-political achievement, every change in the area of labor laws (*Arbeitsrecht*) with respect to labor contracts represents the penetration of the state into the economic sphere quite apart from state management and state monopolies. But the restriction of the liberal idea also occurs within capitalism itself. The trend toward cartels restricts the type of free entrepreneur more and more. A ruling capitalist class comes into existence which is hierarchically organized and which is constituted through cooptation, which assumes a form that is partly modern and partly feudal, and which undermines the authority of the state. The state becomes the instrument of the power of capital (*Kapitalherrschaft*). Its formal independence is preserved in order to bring it all the more easily into actual dependence.

These considerations show that the relation of state and economy cannot be conceived according to either mercantilism or liberalism. But the Romantic classification of the economy as the serving member of the God-state is also not possible. In the sphere of political power, the economy attains an importance very much greater than the position to which it is customarily assigned in an ethical hierarchy of values. The result is, first of all, that the state can never be an economic subject. The freedom of the productive power belongs to the economic as well as to the spiritual process (*Produktion*). The community that has the power of justice is as such not the bearer of the productive powers. But likewise, the state can never be only the external guarantor of an undisturbed production. Otherwise the antinomy of the powers of economic production would, just as the antinomy of spiritual production, destroy the unity of the state, and annul its character as a community that has the power of justice. Here also there is a broken relationship. Political legislation must protect (*Überdecken*) the opposition between the trends and the powers of productivity without dissolving it. Here also a "tacit transfer" must enter in. The state transfers. It retains sovereignty over the economy as well as over education. It defines the goal and the unity of the social formation of production. It does not allow its sovereignty to be snatched away by the capital monopoly of a limited group. It subdues the monopolistic powers that attempt to define the goal of production in the interest of their power. It breaks the dominion of capitalism, and it is able to do so as far as it can rely upon a unified will to production, which alone could be the foundation of a plan of production however it be defined. But the state is not a producer. It transfers the production tacitly to those powers that are able to realize it only in freedom. Here again the word "tacitly" signifies that this act of transfer is not an institution, but only appears in institutions. In this way the tension implied in the concept of transfer remains public. Therefore it is both possible and necessary to fórmulate definitions of the relationship of state and economy which conform to the Protestant principle: definitions that express the fundamental candor of the relationship, also the participation of the state in the meaning of the economy, in its goal and its social structure, and the state's renunciation of its own productivity; in short, definitions that reveal the brokenness and the essential ambiguity of their relationship so that the absolutism of state and economy are overcome by the same principle.

5. THE INTRINSIC FORM OF THE STATE

The community informed by the power of justice needs a real and concrete concentration of power in order to manifest itself as such. Although the state is not identical with this concentration of power, it becomes a reality only through it. Normally, this concentration is identical to the powers that support the structure of the community. The most direct and effective expression of this supporting power of a group is the sacral consecration by which the ruling group creates a sense of conviction in all those subjected to it. It is completely independent of the rational fitness of the individual representative of sovereignty. Not the person, but the office (*Ort*) is holy. Although there can be a conflict of individuals for the office, there can never be a conflict against the office. A particular ruler or a particular aristocracy can be ousted. But the place in which they stand is inviolable.

The situation is entirely different when it is no longer the individual (*der eïnzelne Träger*) but the office itself which is attacked, when the category of "office" in the sense of a static order of powers is brought into question. This is the case in middle-class society. In principle it recognizes no holy office that in itself is inviolable and which makes its fated incumbent inviolable. It recognizes no pre-established hierarchy of powers as the bearing-structure of states. Power is equally distributed to every individual as far as he participates in universal human reason. The actual and concrete exercise of power is in principle transferred, subject to recall. It depends upon the presupposed fitness of the incumbent, and gives him the character of a "functionary," that is, of one who by the commission of all has to perform a special function for all and in the name of all. The functionary has a kind of consecration and inviolability in this sense only, as far as he represents the whole, because the whole, the people, possess something of the consecration of the ancient hierarchies. But even these, and therefore all the structuring powers of society, are denied.

They are denied. They are repressed. Middle-class society cannot leave them as they are, because they are obstacles for economic development. Nevertheless, they are not absent. For reality is organized structurally, it is not egalitarian and structureless. Even in the most extreme democracies, the state is borne by special groups. Their power is concentrated in special offices. But, in a democracy, this is not recognized, legally established, and consecrated, as it is in feudalism. Rather, it remains hidden. It is realized indirectly, without consecration and without law, but therefore no less emphatically. First of all, there are functionaries who somehow always establish themselves in an autonomous ruling structure, frequently constituted through cooptation. Then major-

ity decision is to be construed only as a power struggle that lacks
force but behind which stands the threat of an eventual use of force
by the majority. And finally, functionaries and majorities are in
fact created by the groups that actually bear power; thus, for
example, in capitalist countries by the group that represents the
power of capital (*die Gruppe der Kapitalherrschaft*). Almost without
exception, behind Western democracy stand the great capitalists
as the group that upholds the structure of the state: not unequivocally, frequently divided among themselves, often restricted by
powers that are not yet absorbed by the market, but always present,
and finally always victorious.

It would be false and contrary to the essence of the state as the
justice-bearing community, if one intended simply to condemn
the existence of such structuring powers. But what is to be condemned is that they operate unseen, irresponsibly and indirectly.
Concealed by democracy, they utilize it and undermine it, they bear
it and at the same time destroy it. Up until now, the most effective
opposition against this state of affairs has come from dictatorships.
Dictatorship appears to be the radical antithesis of democracy, but
it is not. Dictatorship is based on democracy. The office of dictator
as such has no consecration. The dictator is a functionary, even
though occasionally or continuously he must disclaim the possibility
of his removal. But the threat, which is given along with the absence
of consecration of the office of dictator, continues to exist. The result
is that the dictator seeks to create a power-bearing group by which
the democracy is structured. The dictator retains a necessary place
within the structure. When this succeeds, then the threat is removed,
and the consecration of the office follows immediately.

But the question is whether something other than an economically
grounded power structure is possible on the basis of capitalistic
democracy, whether the attempt to restore past hierarchies or to
inflate their remains is meaningful or possible. It is characteristic
that the countries where there is a dictatorship, Russia and Italy,
have been affected relatively little by capitalism, that in Russia the
peasantry, and in Italy the middle classes, have a position that is
really [power-]bearing. Here, therefore, an extra-capitalistic structuring is possible up to a certain level. In high-capitalistic countries
this sort of thing is out of the question. Controlling power (*Mächtig-*

keit) lies with the bearers of the capitalistic labor process, and capital and labor struggle for superiority. To look for or to demand a structure independent of this conflict, such as a "national community" (*Volksgemeinschaft*), is romantic, which like all romanticism is secretly in league with the power ruling at the time.

The real power structure should come forth into the open, and responsibly fulfill the position it irresponsibly has usurped. But this does not mean that the state should simply unite itself with this real power structure. Rather, here also, the brokenness of the situation is an expression of the structure of the state corresponding to the spirit of Protestantism. Viewed from this depth, the tension between democracy and the group that bears power is the tension of criticism and realization, of valid demand and the immediate power of being (*Seinsmächtigkeit*), of ideal justice (*Sollensrecht*) and real justice (*Seinsrecht*). The mere power of being (*Seinsmacht*) is demonic and destructive, the mere power of the ideal (*Sollensmacht*) is abstract and vacuous. The essential and intrinsic structure of the state is given in this polarity, that is, in the polarity of the group that gives structure to power (*strukturierende Machtgruppe*) and the democratic corrective. It is important to recognize that in a monarchy aristocratically founded, the position of the monarch frequently includes this democratic element. The monarch, and precisely the absolute monarch, is experienced democratically by an aristocracy that posits itself absolutely. And they are not mistaken, because as representative of the state, he possesses beyond the aristocratic power, which culminates in him, the universal countertendency that subjects the aristocracy to justice. Therefore, the polarity required here is not utopian; rather, it is most profoundly connected with the essence of the realization of political power.

6. THE BASIS OF THE STATE

We have not yet asked about the community that has the power of justice and which bears the state. What kind of community should it be? What, therefore, is the basis of the state? From the standpoints of the questions [treated] thus far, this question could remain temporarily in abeyance, but for our basic theme, the state in expectation and demand, it has fundamental significance. Neverthe-

less, the entire internal structure [of the state] as well as its relationship to spirit and to the economy is largely determined by the
external situation, that is, by the relationship of one self-governing
community (*eine selbstmächtigen Gemeinschaft*) to all the others.
The nation is the state-bearing group appropriate to the present.
The nation-state is the generally prevailing form of political realization. In it arise the tendencies, such as nationalism and imperialism, which raise the immediate will to power of the national
community to the highest principle of social life, unchecked by
encroaching forms of justice. At this point a precarious conflict
arises between power and justice. The community that posits
justice by its intrinsic power (*die ihrer selbst mächtige rechtsetzende
Gemeinschaft*) is sovereign just on account of this function. But so
long as it posits justice, there appears to be no justice posited for
it. The correlation of power and justice appears to be dissolved
in sovereignty. But in this way the solidarity of both, which has
been established by definition, would be destroyed, and the presupposition of the foregoing discussion would become problematic.

The community that is the bearer of justice is a community, that
is to say, the basis of political obligation (*Bindung*) is an immediate
solidarity. Concerning this community, we had defined power and
justice by means of each other. The question now is how to conceive the relationship to those who exist outside the community.
There are three possibilities. The first is, in principle, to recognize
no "outside regions" (*das "Ausserhalb"*). Every group that in fact
exists outside is incorporated into the unity of the state the moment
it enters the horizon, *in potestatem redigitur*. This is the principle
of the naïve imperialistic robber state. In this case, there can be no
question of an antithesis of power and justice, because generally
no externally existing power is recognized, only multitudes and
groups whose legitimacy is denied. The second possibility is to
recognize other groups having the power of justice, but to disclaim
every just relation to them. This is the standpoint of absolute
sovereignty and conscious imperialism. Here also there exists no
antithesis between justice and power. For instance, let us suppose
that a foreign sovereignty is recognized in all seriousness. Then the
power of justice is accordingly attributed to the foreign sovereign
group, and its subjection or restriction is marked by a breach of

justice. On this basis, actual assaults are justified either by making the foreign group responsible for the breach of justice or by claiming that it is essentially incapable of justice and therefore is an object for colonization. Should such an attempt at justification be lacking, then it would be a case of the naïve imperialism of a robber state, and the theory of sovereignty would accordingly be abandoned. When one does not want this then he needs those justifications, demonstrating thereby that he wants to conceive of justice and power as interacting. But the consequence of this thought leads necessarily to a third concept. In this, sovereignty is relativized, and thereby is properly construed only in its consequences. An element of community is posited with the establishment of a foreign sovereignty that points beyond the national or however conditioned basis of the individual state, and which must necessarily find its expression in justice. Expanding justice reveals the elements of the expanding community.

Therefore, it is exactly as it was concerning the internal structure of the state. Every attempt to create an abstract system of justice in which a concrete power group finds no place and which challenges the relative sovereignty of the state and denies the existence of the community that underlies it, is rejected. Rather, it applies here also that justice without a community that has the power of justice is without substance.

Now the question is: Whence does the limitation from absolute to relative sovereignty originate? Here also it must be conceived structurally and not in an egalitarian manner. Within the expanding community of nations which has the power of justice there is a locus (*Ort*) where the power dwelling within it is concentrated, be it specific nations, or—and this is decisive—be it specific homogeneous groups within the nations, as, for example, capitalist leaders or the proletariat. It is fitting that such groups, which determine the structure [of the state], also emerge as externally representative; but also that the opposing tendency that restricts their sovereignty, become effectively manifest. The polarity of criticism and formative power, of what ought to be (*Sollen*) and what is (*Sein*), is valid for the inner structure of the state as well as for the relationship of states to one another.

But this presupposes the present existence of community and of elements of expanding intrinsic power (*Selbsmächtigkeit*) between the communities that up until now were confined to the sovereign states. No fundamental decision has been made concerning what exists in this respect in the present or what is possible in the future. Certainly "humanity" as the ultimate community that has the power of justice is as little utopian as were the great nation-states before they arose. Rather, it is the inevitable consequence of the transition from the naïve robber state to the recognition in principle of foreign sovereignties. Because the sphere in which decisions concerning justice are made must become more universal as the community that posits justice becomes more comprehensive, there remains in the growth of this kind of universal political order (*in solch universaler Verstaatlichung*) the greatest breadth for relative sovereignty in all concrete spheres—a possibility that is indeed realized even now within the expanding unity of the great nation states. On the basis of the tension between the ruling power groups and the expanding unity, a graded structure of the relative power of justice is conceivable in which power as justice and justice as power become actual and together reveal the concrete and universal community.

It is clear that such a community is possible only on the basis of a source of meaning (*Sinngebung*) that creates unity at the ultimate level of being. According to its essence, the church is the group that represents and bears this ultimate source of meaning. The following principle can be derived from this: political unity can extend only as far as church unity. This principle, on which medieval state-church politics is based is true, when it is interpreted not as it was in the Middle Ages, but in a Protestant way: when the church is only the church in polarity with the autonomous spirituality that limits it, and when, therefore, the church always stands dialectically toward its own form and existence, when the church always stands above itself. But when this is so, then the Protestant conception of the state conquers the humanistic conception of the state founded on reason, the pagan conception of the national robber state, and the Catholic conception of the state subject to the concrete church. The consciousness of the brokenness of every human state of being that informs Protestantism leads it to a broken and, just for that reason, true conception of the state.

Shadow and Substance:
A Theory of Power*

1

In the announcement of this conference I found that my address stands under four titles: a general one, "Commitment of Freedom"; a particular one, "The Price and the Opportunity of Power"; a challenging one, "Shadow and Substance"; and a problematic one, "The Relevance of Christian Ethics to the Use of Power." And I myself have added a fifth one: "The Universality and the Integrity of Power." The abundance of titles shows both the significance and the difficulty of the problems to be discussed. It also points to the interdependence of freedom, power, and love—love being the ultimate principle of Christian ethics.

In meditating about concepts like freedom, power, justice, and love, and their relationship to each other, one finds that the first thing one must do in order to penetrate into their substance is purge them of many levels of dust, heaped upon them by political rhetoric, distorting propaganda, and daily-life superficiality. It is a hard but continuously necessary job, a task through which the philosopher and the theologian can help men of active politics to make their decisions with more awareness of the ethical presuppositions and the humane good of every political action.

* Originally written in English as lecture delivered at the Graduate School of the Department of Agriculture, Washington, D.C., May 7, 1965.

After such deductions have been accomplished, one often sees relationships between elements of the life-process which were hidden before and are surprising when rediscovered, for example, relations between power and love—our particular forms.

When one speaks of power in relation to Christian ethics, one should always remember that the most frequent way of addressing God in prayer is to call him "Almighty God," and that it is just this unconditional power of being which characterizes God as God, a fact that makes it impossible to speak of power as if it were evil in itself.

If we look in the light of this basic religious assertion at the processes of life, we find that there is power of being, the power of resisting the threat of nonbeing, for all beings from the atom to the human person. Each of them, too, has a center and a manifoldness of elements united by it, like the nucleus of the atom and the electrons around it or the conscious, knowing, and deciding ego in the individual man and the manifoldness of memories, desires, and thoughts in him. Man has the greatest power of being among all things on earth, because he looks at the universe and calls it universe and can unite with every part of it in knowledge and action. Therefore, he has been called the "image of God" by the Old Testament and the "small universe" by the philosophers of the Renaissance. The greatness of this power has become manifest as never before in man's ability to liberate himself from total bondage to the ground out of which he has grown, the earth; but also in his possibility of destroying himself along with all life on earth. He can surpass and he can annihilate a large part, perhaps the most important part, of the divine creation on earth.

But the occasion of this conference calls for the consideration of another kind of power, namely, that of the social group. I intentionally say "another kind of power." For one must, from the very beginning, avoid a wrong analogy between the individual person and the social group. The social group does not have what the developed person has: a natural center of thought, deliberation, and decision. In spite of all seeming analogies, no government, not even the most democratically chosen, has the same relation to the members of the group as the personal center has for the whole person in acts of responsible decision. My left hand is not excused if my right hand commits murder. But there are millions of Germans who were not guilty of the murders committed by Hitler in the name of the German people. There is certainly a responsibility in the fact that he acquired the power to commit his crimes, a responsibility shared not only by every German but also by all Fascist- and Nazi-minded people in other countries, including America, who helped to pave his way to power. But this does not make all of them guilty of what has been done by the German dictator.

Neither a nation nor any other social group has a personal center. Therefore both this power of being and this moral responsibility have another character than that of an individual person. There is a combination of natural and personal elements. Every social group, like every living being, affirms itself and its own being, internally against destructive elements and externally against hostile forces. On the other hand, every social group, in contrast to other natural structures, consists of persons with a morally responsible center. This is the reason for the profound problem of social ethics, which appeared in the earliest discussion of Christian theologians and continues to appear in contemporary pronouncements of Christian councils and lectures of professors of social ethics. And this is the reason the Christian churches always have been attacked by people who are unable to accept a solution that is not an unambiguous Yes or No but which shows the intricacies of everything alive. If they see *only* the fact that a social group consists of morally responsible persons, they support that type of pacifism which demands total resignation of power—an act which an individual person always can do and in certain situations should do—but which disregards the natural basis of social existence. If, on the other hand, they see *only* the natural self-affirmation of a social group they support a militarism which, in the name of the power or the prestige of, for example, a nation, disregards the difference between a community of men and a predatory animal. Readiness of defense becomes the covering name for readiness to attack, and the so-called "interests" that must be defended offer an excellent means of blurring the boundary-line between defense and attack.

The last remark forces us back to a consideration of what the power-of-being of a social group really means. It means, first of all, centeredness in the political sense—that is, the possibility of acting with *one* will, even if this will is forced by the ruling powers upon the majority of the members against their own will. The other condition of the power of a social group is its having a space and being able to keep it, against both inner disintegration and outer aggression. The third condition of political power is the possibility of growth, for as a natural being it cannot live without growth. This is the most frequent reason for the willful as well as the tragically inescapable conflicts of social powers. Before discussing these points in light of the estrangement of man from his true being, I want to show the relation of love to power in the sense we have defined it. It seems surprising, but it must be stated that power as power is one with love. Such an assertion implies, even requires, a desentimentalization of the concept of love. This is a hard task, partly because there is only one word for "love" in modern languages, against four words in Greek, distinguishing the different characteristics love can have; partly because the emotional element in some forms of love is so strong that it produces passionate reactions against any attempt to show its nonemotional basis. But there *is* such a basis, namely, the drive of everything separated toward that to which it belongs. Love is the urge for the reunion of the separated. It is a universal love for everything that exists. And wherever power supports such reunion, power performs the work of love. It does so in all small or large communities; in a flock of birds, in a family, in a town, in a tribe, in a nation, in the unity for which we are hoping—the unity of mankind and, above this, the universal reunion of everything that is, in its divine "Ground and Aim," called in Christianity the kingdom of God. In all of them, to the degree to which they are what they are supposed to be, love and power are united. A third element is present, without which love would not be love, nor would power be power. Its name is "justice," a word which needs purgation as much as the other two words. Justice is the structure of power without which power would be destructive, and it is the backbone of love without which love would be sentimental self-surrender. In both of them it is the principle of form and measure. Formless love wastes the person who loves and abuses the person who is loved; and formless power destroys, first, other centers of power, and then itself. This is the reason religion praises the justice of God and demands the justice of man, and speaks even of the covenant God has made not only with nations but also with the trees and the animals. Today this covenant is treated in lectures on ecology, the balanced ways of natural growth. And the answer to the question, What is justice in man? is first given by descriptions of the sociological structures of a society and the psychological structures of human beings generally. It is the justice in power and the justice in love that is sought in such inquiries, whether the inquirer realizes it or not. They help to fulfill the oldest and always renewed demands of religion generally and Christian ethics in particular. It is what I would call creative justice and would identify with love.

2

We have suggested that the relationship between love and power and of both of them to justice is in reality not what it essentially is, and therefore ought to be in human existence. We have discussed and purified important concepts and we have shown their essential or true relation. But we did not show what the relationship of the things they designate actually is. So far, our consideration has been intentionally abstract, because without such basic discussion everything said later would remain an opinion of the speaker but not a valid argument, whether accepted or not. It is the dignity and the burden of philosophy to ask for the hidden assumptions of a political view, and in doing so to delve into the structures of all life.

But now we must turn to the realities of human existence, which is an estranged reality, estranged, for example, from that unity of power and love in the form of justice which is the basis for all valuation of power. We considered earlier a distorted love that is neither just to others nor to the one who loves. We must now think of that character of power from which all its distortions follow. It is a fact that power implies the possibility of coercion, the threat of the application of force. And it is not only a possibility and a threat, but also a tragically unavoidable reality in the existence of the human race. It is applied in all three directions in which the power of a social group is actual. It is applied in the establishment and protection of a united will of the social group. It breaks the resistance of individuals or particular groups by enforcing the law. And coercion is used in settling and defending the space which is the given or chosen place of this group, space not only in the geographical sense but also in the sense of social and cultural traditions, of ideas and hopes. Neither assimilation nor education, neither political nor military defense is possible without measures of coercion. And, finally, force is applied when, in the process of change and extension, of growth and disintegration, one centered social group encounters another one. If we ask how reality would look if in the long evolution from plant to animal, from animal to man, from primitive to present-day man, from small family-like groups to national and supernational unities, coercion had not been applied, no amount of imagination could give an answer. But where there is force there is injustice. The essential unity of love and power is destroyed—but not totally! Otherwise, life could not have survived on earth. Not only in man, but also in nature it would have destroyed itself. We live from the elements of justice, which counterbalance the injustice implied in the use of force. This makes every life-process ambiguous. It is never only good or only evil. It separates for the sake of a higher union. It unites to prepare a deeper cleavage.

This is the reason life in all its dimensions, in nature as well as in history, can never be judged with simple moral concepts. Nothing in it is unambiguously good or bad. We certainly must judge, but only with the awareness that what we judge, in the same moment judges us. This is so when we have to scold our children, and their sad or hostile expressions reproach us. It is so when we have to punish the criminal and feel that his suffering is not only his own affair, but that there is in it an element of suffering for our indirect participation in his guilt. And it is so when we have to answer the application of military force with military force, and become aware that once more the unity of power and love is disrupted through innumerable smaller or larger actions on all sides which have led, perhaps over long periods, to the final break. We have to apply force; otherwise we would sacrifice that power in which love is embodied, we would sacrifice that justice which is the principle of form of all social life. In all this the unavoidable and the tragic character of coercion is obvious.

Why is coercion tragic? Because it transforms the object of coercion, at least partly, into a thing, into a mere object that is deprived of *its* spontaneity, of its living response; or, in the case of a person, he is deprived of *his* freedom to act out of the totality of his being. A law that is not the expression of his identity is imposed upon him. With that part of his personal existence upon which force is exercised he has ceased to be personal and therefore able to have a full community with other persons. This is the terrible thing in every coercion—not the pain it produces, but the partial depersonalization that is connected with the application of force. And this is true not only of him who is forced, but also of him who forces. And it is even true if we have to force ourselves into the repression of elements that belong to us as living beings.

This structure of coercion may explain a phenomenon that has been a riddle at all times but of which we have become aware only in the twentieth century. It is the partly unconscious projection of an image of "the enemy" which has nothing to do with reality but which as image has a demonic-destructive function in persons and groups. The enemy is seen as less than human; he shows all the characteristics of evil, murder, and deceit that the Fourth Gospel ascribes to the devil. Therefore no community with him is possible. And the tragic implication of coercion is removed. One does not need to suffer when one applies coercion to him. There is no guilt on the side of him who exercises force even to the point of total destruction against such enemy. In order to fulfill this function, the enemy must be concrete and easily identifiable. This lies behind the image of the Jewish character in Nazi Germany, behind the image of the bourgeoisie in present-day Russia, behind the image of the communist conspiracy in America. These images liberate one from any hesitation and restriction in the application of force. They themselves are, of course, products of the anxiety over becoming a mere object within mass society, and of the desire to resist this destiny by transforming others into mere objects. Since they are products of a lack of power they attempt to provide for power by resort to force. Genuine power knows the tragic, though unavoidable, character of coercive force.

3

The question now arises whether love, in order to overcome the tragic implications of power, should demand the resignation of power altogether. The picture of Jesus shows that the resignation of power can be the greatest power—if the situation demands it. But even of him it was not always demanded. Power through resignation of power is a human possibility, for which one uses the term "spiritual power." That kind of power cannot use force, for every spiritual influence is received in the totality of our person and presupposes a free, deliberating, and deciding center. Not even God can force anybody spiritually; and if human beings try it, they fail, because they confuse psychological coercion with the communication of the spirit. All churches are in danger of this confusion. Their spiritual power diminishes exactly to the degree in which they apply coercive power. They may have a strong political, social, and cultural grip on their members and on a whole society, not only through ecclesiastical authorities, as in Catholicism, but also through social pressures, as in the churches in "suburban captivity," to borrow a recent phrase. But each of these forms of coercion reduces the spiritual power of the churches.

This leads to the problem of the resignation of coercive power by a nation. At the beginning of this address we denied that one can call a social group a person. The natural center is lacking. From this follows that no nation should surrender its existence in time and space voluntarily. It can accept changes in its spatial basis, it can enter into larger unities, it can divide itself into smaller parts. But it cannot deny itself. It must use force and take upon itself the tragic consequences for itself and for others of such use. But it must remain aware of these consequences and of the ultimate unity of love and power. It must reject the agitators who produce the image of an enemy who is nothing but enemy, and it must remember that force should never be the tool of hatred, but always the tragically unavoidable way of love to conquer what is against love, and to create the ultimate unity of what belongs together.

Is there, we must now ask, a place where the tragic necessity of coercion is overcome? The answer of Christian ethics is: not in time and space. It is always possible to overcome particular occasions for the use of coercion, but there is no abolition of this necessity altogether. Human existence does not permit the utopia of power lacking all compelling force. It does not exist in nature outside man; it does not exist in nature inside man. It comes to fulfillment only above the processes of life, in eternity. But the processes of life are directed toward that which they never can reach. And so continuously new situations appear in which force must be used, in different ways, and it is the wisdom of love, united with power, to employ it in obedience to the requirement of the situation.

Rarely has there been a change of such momentum as that brought about by the invention of nuclear weapons. Force as the tool of power united with love in the form of justice has become the means of the destruction of all human power. The amount of change that is the consequence of this cannot be fully realized by us upon whom it fell without inner preparation for it. Certainly it does not change the ultimate principles of Christian ethics or the ultimate aim of human life and history. Neither does it remove the tragic necessity of coercion. But it changes—and probably more radically than we realize—the ways in which power uses force in the service of love. In some way it is the end of war in the traditional meaning of the word. If its coercive strength is fully used it does not coerce but annihilates him who uses it and him against whom it is used. The aim of power to unite and to do what love wants is denied by the eradication of bearers of power. A war without a possible victor and a possible reunion of the separated is not a war but merely a catastrophe. We do not know whether this catastrophe approaches. Chrisian ethics does not deny the right to a defense with equal tools against anybody who would use these tools. But Christian ethics denies to anybody the right to use these tools in such a way as to contravene the divine creation and the future potentialities of human history. Force serves power; but if it destroys power in serving it, it contradicts its own meaning.

In this address I have tried to show that power does not contradict Christian ethics, or, beyond this, the universal ethics of love. I have attempted to overcome the schism between the world in which coercive force is necessary and the world in which the law of love is valid. These are not two worlds, but one—the one world in whose divine ground, power and love are united; in which power and love, in their coexistence, conflict in a thousand ways, yet whose hope is the reunion of power and love—fragmentarily, in history, but complete only, beyond time and space.

The Political Meaning of Utopia*

1. THE ROOT OF UTOPIA IN MAN'S BEING

When the word "utopia" is heard and used in ordinary daily speech, the thought may frequently occur that to characterize something as utopian is to dub it as nonsense, and for many people utopia and nonsense are not very different. Utopia is believed to be a fantastic representation of things that never become reality. No adherent of *Realpolitik,* in the Bismarckian sense of the term, can afford to concern himself with anything of this sort. The fact, however, that such a large assembly** as this finds itself for four evenings debating the problem of utopia and the fact that the directors of the Hochschule für Politik have considered this theme sufficiently worthy to place their facilities and resources at its disposal show that utopia must be something other than nonsense. But if utopia is something other than worthless fantasy, it must have a foundation in the structure of man himself, for in the last analysis only that has significance which has a foundation in the structure of man. If it did not have this, it could be viewed as nothing but the projection of wishful thinking, for example, or as a sociological phenomenon valid in certain periods but not in others. Or it could be considered as something transitory and dispensable, as something incompatible with the seriousness of *Realpolitik* which consequently must be destroyed as harmful. But if this is not so, if it belongs

---

* Translated by William R. Crout, Walter Bense and James L. Adams.
** The following four lectures were delivered at the Deutsche Hochschule für Politik in Berlin in the summer of 1951.

to man's being to think in utopian forms, then things are different. Then utopia is not something that can be eliminated but something that endures as long as man endures. And I believe this to be the case.

I believe it can be shown that utopia has a foundation in man's being, and since man's being is representative of being in general, this means that utopia has its basis in being in general. For this reason I consider it a matter of considerable import, though it will probably astonish many of you, that I undertake an analysis of a political concept with an examination of those aspects of man which necessarily, according to man's essence, give rise to the formation of utopias. This does not mean that I shall speak today exclusively in an ontological or, in the deeper sense of the word, anthropological way. I want to point out political implications as we go along, but our fundamental concern must be first with man as man and, subsequently, with man as a historical being, for these are the two basic analyses we must carry out in order not to speak about utopia and politics as political dogmatists or as agitators. To speak seriously about a subject means to speak from its root, and the root of all things lies ultimately in man's essence and in the ground of being insofar as it reveals itself to man. The first order of thought must therefore be to investigate that side of man which is responsible for utopia and for which I would like to use the term "finite freedom."

If asked, "How would you define man in a couple of words?" I would answer: "As finite freedom." The combination of the two terms "finitude" and "freedom" conveys such a richness of ontological and anthropological connotations that I cannot go into them all; I believe, however, that when these two words are combined the position of man as man is grasped and properly expressed. A few words, then, about these two concepts, freedom and finitude.

Freedom here is not at all meant in the sense of the debate between determinism and indeterminism, between the doctrine of "freedom of the will" and "bondage of the will." I consider this debate obsolete, as something that should no longer be engaged in because it is clear that it proceeds from assumptions that make the decision for determinism unavoidable from the outset and that transform indeterminism into a protest without giving real understanding. What I mean by freedom is something utterly different, something given in our immediate experience, in the awareness of each one of us, namely, two things. First, that man is able to act as a whole person, as a self in the wholeness of his being, and that only when he can do this does he experience the phenomenon for which all languages have used the term "freedom" or analogous words. This is not a matter dependent on a solution to the problem of determinism *vs.* indeterminism, but a phenomenon of which we are aware whenever we look at ourselves apart from all theoretical bias. Then we find that we are unfree to the extent that we discover divided tendencies in us, and free to the extent that we act as whole persons. This is the first thing I mean by the concept of freedom. The second is "having possibilities." A friend of mine, the neurologist [Kurt] Goldstein, once said: *"Man is that being which has possibility,"* without saying possibility for what, and that is precisely the excellence of this definition. Man does not have possibility for something definite but, in contradistinction to all other creatures, he has "possibility"; he is that being which is able to transcend the given, and infinitely to transcend it. There is nothing given that man is not able, in principle, to transcend. That he cannot in fact do so is the problem of finitude. But he has the possibility of doing so, and having possibility is the second thing I mean by freedom, and it is this that must be understood in order to understand what is contained in the concept of utopia.

If I now ask, "Why is unfreedom so dehumanizing? Why do we struggle so for freedom and defend it as we do?" we must go back for a reply to the foundation of man's being and derive the answer from there. We do not experience *unfreedom* as dehumanizing because we are deprived of definite possibilities but because we are no longer able to react as whole persons. And this is the reason the struggle for freedom is a struggle for man himself and not for something belonging to man. He who no longer is able to act from centeredness, from wholeness, whence all elements of his being join in an ultimate decision, has ceased to be man in the true sense of the world. He is dehumanized; and it is very important that we understand clearly that the concept of dehumanization derives from this phenomenon of unfreedom. The point is not that we are deprived of possibilities, that we cannot travel, that we cannot go wherever we want to go (many sick people cannot do this), or that we cannot say whatever we want to say (where can that be done? Not even in the family is that possible). But the question is, are we able to react as whole persons? If that is no longer possible, if our central "I" is transformed into an object incapable of reacting in a centered way, then the process of dehumanization has begun. I therefore believe that the root of unfreedom, one of the most fundamental concepts, is shown by such an ontological analysis.

One further point about possibility. The concept of possibility is identical with the concept of *temptation*. Possibility is temptation. In the life of the individual, it is clear that man is truly man because he can be tempted. In the biblical myth, immediately after man steps forth as man he is tempted—in other words, an appeal is made to him who "has possibility." The serpent does not itself experience temptation; it does what it must, it is cunning and acts in a cunning way (of course I am speaking mythically); it tempts neither trees nor animals nor God, but man. It is man alone who has possibility, and temptation is the appeal to possibility. But at the same time this appeal expresses the fact that man is truly man; could he not be tempted he would cease to be man.

Let me immediately apply this to politics, where there is exactly the same phenomenon. You know the famous saying that power corrupts whoever has power. You not only know it, you have experienced it. Why does power corrupt? Because power can be defined as having possibility in a concrete, practical sense. That which ontologically constitutes man's nature—his having possibility—becomes a concrete possibility in an organization or group that has power and this is why politics is a place where temptation is magnified. But in power lies also the *dignity of politics,* just as in man's capacity to be tempted lies his dignity and risk. Dignity and risk are always correlates.

This is one aspect of freedom, but because freedom is finite there is another. Man is finite freedom. What does *finitude* mean? It means that when man actualizes his possibility on the basis of a totally integrated response, that is, on the basis of freedom, he is then threatened—*threatened by nonbeing,* for finitude is the mixture of being and nonbeing. At every moment we are in the situation of this mixture of being and nonbeing. Nonbeing is not something at which we can look as though it were outside us. At every moment we are in nonbeing just as much as in being—at every moment we are threatened. Here we should not only think of death and of all the contingencies that may bring it, but also of that nonbeing which shows itself as error and guilt. Our freedom to actualize possibilities beyond everything given is at the same time what threatens us as finite beings.

Let me again apply this to politics and speak of the threat to political existence, for political existence, like human existence in general, is threatened by nonbeing. Is there an unthreatened existence? Occasionally churches have maintained that inasmuch as they have a religious foundation they have an unthreatened—because unpolitical—existence which is expressed in the symbol of "Eternal Rome." Somewhat more modest is Toynbee's idea that those Christian nations who belong to the Anglican tradition, that is, to a certain synthesis of Protestantism and Catholicism, have a guarantee that their political existence is unthreatened. Others have based similar claims on an alleged racial or ideological superiority. But in each instance one side of man's finite freedom, the side of finitude, of nonbeing, has disappeared. For history has shown and will continue to show even to the churches and to Christian culture that political existence is necessarily and inevitably a threatened existence. Like everything human, it is threatened by nonbeing.

If we proceed from these assumptions, we can understand that this finite freedom, which man is, expresses itself in two elements that belong to man at every moment, namely, in a constantly unstable *balance of anxiety and courage*. Man's being, by virtue of nonbeing, of finitude, of being threatened, is in anxiety at every moment, and it affirms itself, takes its anxiety upon itself; and what that means, this city [Berlin] has certainly come to know. Man's being accepts his anxiety, does not attempt to deny it or overlook it, but on the contrary does what the word "courage" means, namely, says Yes to being despite the threat of nonbeing.

Political existence manifests the same character of anxiety and courage in relation to the present and the future. Let me again examine these concepts and apply them to politics. *Anxiety is an ontological concept*—that is, it does not denote something accidental, which one may or may not have, which one may or may not overcome. Anxiety is a synonym for finitude; it is finitude seen from within. Because we are finite, anxiety is not a phenomenon that might perchance be dispelled by trumpet blasts; neither can it be removed, as neurotic anxiety can be, by psychoanalysis, nor as the anxiety of guilt, through forgiveness; but ontological anxiety is nothing other than our awareness that we are finite. We become aware of it at certain moments. Though we are not always anxious, anxiety is always there, just as nonbeing and finitude are always there. It is exceedingly important that we affirm and not deny this anxiety. Nothing is more dangerous, even politically dangerous, than to believe that one can avoid it by turning away from it. There is only one way to confront anxiety (and I shall have something to say about this in connection with religion)—namely, to take it upon oneself. Taking anxiety upon oneself is not saying, "Now I am without it." The man of courage is not without anxiety, but he takes his anxiety upon himself. The man who is not fully self-aware may in certain moments be without anxiety—like the sergeant who said to the intellectual, "You are full of anxiety," and to whom the intellectual replied, "Sergeant, if you had as much anxiety as I, you would have turned and run long ago." Courage is not the absence of anxiety but the taking of anxiety upon oneself, namely, to face nothingness and nevertheless say Yes to the ground of being from which we come.

If one cannot do this there arises the phenomenon of neurotic anxiety. *Neurotic anxiety* is a result of failing to take this ontological anxiety upon oneself—the anxiety in which we all are one, which is identical with our finitude. When related to the present, ontological anxiety becomes the *will to security,* which gives rise to aggression against threats of every kind. This is one of the elemental phenomena of politics; anxiety, for instance, through the will to security and aggressiveness, which are inseparably connected, produced the World War. As basis of the will to security, anxiety has necessarily the consequence of producing the very thing it seeks to avoid by the way it tries to avoid it. We experience this now on a world–wide scale as never before.

For this reason the phenomenon of anxiety is of fundamental significance for all politics. In domestic politics, it produces the will to security, which seeks always to safeguard against future threats by becoming all the more attached to the past. This is particularly true now in America. Within all political groups and movements, much of the will to security is a product of anxiety, which returns to the past, choosing it rather than the present or the future because it believes it will find in the past, which, after all, it has survived, securities that are unthreatened. But even this involves a certain courage. Will to security is not simply something that must be rejected; self-protection is a form of courage. The question is only whether the other side of courage, the dimension of the future, is not thereby forgotten.

This brings me to another category, that of *expectation,* and this category presents immediately the problem of utopia. Anxiety and courage are both present in expectation, not in relation to the past, however, but to the future. Expectation looks to the fulfillment in the future of those possibilities which indeed constitute the essence of man. There are always possibilities that may remain unfulfilled— infinite possibilities, owing to the infinite capacity of man to transcend every conditioned situation. But man has courage—as Nietzsche rightly said, he is the most courageous animal—because he expectantly goes forward beyond the given, toward the future.

Let me say something here about *anxiety and expectation.* Expectation includes two anxieties. One anxiety is that in moving out of the past into the future and giving up that which has proved stabilizing, security will be lost—and nothing can live without security. Yet if one pulls back from the future under threat of this loss, there arises another anxiety, namely, that of losing possibilities for the future. This double anxiety may be clarified by the *psychology of innocence.* Innocence—and sexual innocence is the clearest and the most universally known example—is characterized by a double form of anxiety. On one side is anxiety over going forward, the anxiety of confronting the mysterious and unknown in expectation, the anxiety that does not know what will happen if the security of innocence is surrendered. On the other side is the anxiety that by remaining innocent one should lose one's possibilities, the anxiety of nonfulfillment which impels us forward beyond innocence. Innocence stands between these two anxieties and in this situation of anxiety, it has to make a decision. But when it makes its decision it is no longer innocent, not even if it decides for nonactualization, because its immediacy is in any case lost as the result of a conscious decision.

This is true of man's situation in relation to the future, and it is exactly the same in politics. Each of us in all areas of life, especially in the areas that converge in politics, stands before the question of how far he can and should go beyond the securities provided by the past, the institutions in which we live. If we choose not to go beyond them, we experience the anxiety of losing our possibilities and remaining confined in the prison of the past; we feel that new possibilities will pass us by. If, on the other hand, we choose to go beyond the securities and the institutions of the past, we experience, and ought to experience, the *anxiety of revolution.* Here I would add that the courage of the revolutionists, the professional revolutionaries, is just like that of the sergeant who did not take his anxiety upon himself because he had not yet attained to the full measure of being human. There is a revolutionary pathos, however, which takes this risk upon itself and has the courage to say Yes despite the threat of nonbeing and despite the loss of the security provided by the past.

These remarks have been an attempt to delve a little into the human foundations of which all of us are, in some measure, aware. These things cannot be deduced in the form of an abstract ontology, but they nevertheless constitute man's being; we see them at every moment both in ourselves and around us in the explosive and creative reality of politics. It is good occasionally to be challenged to look to the root of all this. What is the source of our courage? What is true courage? This word has been greatly abused. In German "courage," *Mut,* is related to "mind" or "feeling," *Gemüt;* it is not a separate virtue but a central concept. Life's possibility of saying Yes to itself goes far beyond a particular concept, and the same is true of anxiety. Anxiety is not something unusual but a basic phenomenon. Despite its infinite variations—it can become neurosis, guilt, tragedy—it always remains anxiety. The significance of this fact for the political situation is incalculable. But its particular application would require endless analysis and I must now turn to something else.

We have spoken of the past, from which we derive our securities, of the future, in which we give them up, and of the stress and strain between the conservative and the revolutionary forms of anxiety and courage. Now I would like to ask: When we go forward into the future, when we attempt to actualize our possibilities, what are we envisaging? How do we visualize that toward which we are moving?

To answer I must speak now about the *ideal structures* that result from this anticipation or expectation and which have a remarkable characteristic, namely, that they are not simply projected into the future but are likewise found in the past. One of the most important insights into the essence of utopia is that every utopia creates a foundation for itself in the past—that there are backward-looking utopias just as there are forward-looking ones. In other words, that which is envisioned as the ideal in the future is at the same time that which is projected as "once upon a time" in the past—or as that from which one comes and to which one seeks to return. It is one of the most astonishing phenomena of human thought that in all symbol-systems—religious, mythical, political, aesthetic—past and future are correlates, that the source of the past and the goal of the future corresponds to each other. Why is this? Again, because of the will to security. That which points to the future, and is expected to be consummated in the future, is seen as already having been present in the past, as that which corresponds to man's essence. This the German language shows in the cognate relation of *Wesen* (essence) and *gewesen* (been). One of its deepest insights is the apprehension that "essence" (*Wesen*) is that from which we come and which has always been. The same insight is found in Aristotle, who expressed it with the difficult concept τὸ τί ἦν εἶναι.

This accounts for the *phenomenon of the backward-looking utopia,* which is found universally in all mythologies and frequently in philosophy as well. *Dreams of a better life*—as Ernst Bloch entitled one of his writings—are primarily dreams that look in the first instance to the past, but then also to the future. In other words, the warrant for dreaming of the better life to come is derived from the fact that the content of these dreams was once reality. I need mention only a few names to make this clear: the Stoic concept of the Golden Age, which lies in the past and yet will come again after the world-conflagration; the Indian idea of different cosmic ages of which ours is the worst, though the return of the primordial age is imminent; the Christian symbol of the lost paradise, which in analogous symbols in the last book of the Bible is envisioned as restored at the End of Days; Rousseau's ideas about an original pure state of nature which is corrupted by culture and to which man must return; the utopia of original Communism, which is mentioned, to be sure, only incidentally and very cautiously by Marx himself but which has been fully carried through by others and is the basis for the classless society of the future; and countless other myths of which I need take no notice because they all manifest the same structure of a time of origin [*Urzeit*] and a time of the end [*Endzeit*].

The deepest reason for this is that "essence" is seen as belonging to the time of origin, that the essence of man or the essence of being as such is believed to have been realized "in the beginning" and subsequently to have been lost, that although we now exist in contradiction to it, it can be restored to its original state. As a philosopher I would say that the ontological distinction between *essence* and *existence, essence* and *actuality,* is here projected into the dimension of time. Essence (*Wesen*) is conceived as "that which has been" (*das Gewesene*), as that which once "was" (*gewest*), when there was as yet no difference between essence and existence. Then came existence, the "fall," and this existence is now the antithesis, the disruption, the negation of the original unity of the essential and the actual. The result is that the overwhelming majority of these utopias show a triadic movement: the original actualization, namely, actualization of the essence; a falling away from this original actualization, namely, the present condition; and the restoration as an expectation that which has fallen away from its primordial condition is to be recovered. One of the distinguishing characteristics of this triadic movement is the consciousness on the part of those who use this symbolism—almost without exception—that the lowest point of the falling away has been reached in their time, in the moment in which they themselves live. It is always the last period that gives birth to utopia. Illustrative of this, and perhaps also the best formula that has been given for it, is Joachim di Fiore's idea that we live in the Age of consummate sinfulness. Also illustrative is Augustine's idea that the world empires have come to an end with the last one, the great Roman empire which he as a Roman loved, and that their sole successor is to be the kingdom of God, which is in some measure actualized in the church but whose final actualization will take place only after the close of history. The same idea is found in India, where it is always the last period in which the theologian who speaks of a succession of ages finds himself; in Greece, where the Stoics speak about the Iron Age, the last, the most wicked; in Marxism, where the class struggle, running through the whole of history, is seen to have reached a point where revolutionary change has become inevitable because without it the human situation would move beyond all hope of redemption; in the biologic-fascistic ideologies, where decline, *decadence* (Nietzsche), has reached its final stage, where a counter-movement must set in. All of these instances show that the triadic progression is centered on the moment in which the reversal is immediately imminent. This is characteristic of all utopian thought.

Before going into further detail, I would like to make a few comments about the types of thinking in which restoration from this state of total fallenness can be conceived. But first, two types must be mentioned which regard such a restoration as impossible.

The first of these is represented by classical theology where the fall of man results in the subjection of the empirical world to demonic tragic powers, or structures of compulsion as they are analogously described in psychology. Just as the patient can do nothing against his compulsions, man as man can do nothing against these powers, so that within history deliverance in the ontological sense is impossible. This is the idea of the bondage of the will, of being unfree in the religious sense, which Luther fought out with Erasmus and as Augustine did with Pelagius. It is the idea that the demonic powers that rule in the condition of fallenness—and "demonic" here refers to "structure of destruction"—cannot be overcome in history.

The second type, related to the first yet very different, is that of the contemporary existentialists who, unlike nineteenth-century existentialists such as Kierkegaard, Nietzsche, Marx, Dilthey and his school, Bergson, and others, contribute nothing positive to counter their negative analyses. Of course I mean Heidegger and Sartre and a certain tendency in American pragmatism and naturalism. For these thinkers no restoration is possible because there is no "true being" of man, no "essence" from which man has fallen. What we see as man's fallenness they see as man himself, and to call his condition "fallen" is, they believe, to commit from the outset a philosophical error. Sartre's saying, "Man's essence is his existence"—if it had been understood and had not been rendered innocuous by being so abstract—is scarcely less momentous than Nietzsche's proclamation that in modern culture God is dead. Both are saying that there is no longer a realm of embracing values, a true and good structure of being. That was what Nietzsche meant when he declared that God is dead, and this makes him, in a sense, the father of existential philosophy. It is not the childish idea of a foolish atheist; Nietzsche is not to be interpreted so absurdly. It means, rather, that the system of value which has its root in the idea of God has collapsed and that consequently man must create new values himself, out of his own existence. These can have no validity, however, and ultimately remain without criterion. Sartre's statement that man's existence is his essence means that every moment of his existence he creates essence for himself, but that there is no transcendent order from which his existence could be criticized. Hence there can be no utopia; and among the existentialists and those who resemble them, you will find a complete absence of utopia wherever these principles are adopted with radical seriousness.

Nietzsche himself, who belongs to the nineteenth century, did not draw the same inference. In contradiction to his own conception he developed a kind of biologic essentialism that was as mischievous as his own thinking was faulty. All this has been known for a long time but must be mentioned here because it has had great political consequences. In any case, both of these currents of thought, the classical Christian and the radical existentialist of the twentieth century, are agreed that no utopia is possible because the concept of essence has been abandoned. I have at times been struck by the surprising similarity in this respect between the formulations of Barth and Sartre. Were I to point it out to them, both would probably be offended since neither is very fond of the other. Yet the similarity is there and it is in this sense that Barth is to be included among the existentialist theologians, since his theology rejects the humanistic doctrine that essential man is still present after the fall

—however corrupt or paradoxical this presence may be. Both thinkers are basically antihumanistic, even though Sartre has written a
book, *Existentialism is a Humanism,* in which he seeks, albeit weakly,
to vindicate himself. Existentialism is not a humanism, nor is
Barthian theology when its principles are carried through in a
radical way. Having mentioned Barth here, I would like to take the
opportunity to acknowledge his genius: he has the merit of being
truly no Barthian. The reader of his history of Protestant theology
which contains among other things a philosophy of art, perceives
that he is a humanist. But Barth will not admit it.

If one could restore the very much misused word "humanism" to
its proper greatness and significance, one might say: humanism is
the belief that man is determined by his essence, which has not been
absolutely lost and which endures over against existence as judgment
and norm, even in the greatest aberrations of existence. Every politics that does not have this doctrine of man's essence must necessarily
be destructive. To say this is already to speak for utopia. From belief in the essence of man, in that "which has been from all time,"
arises the norm that utopia provides as an image projected into the
future.

There are thus two currents of thought, one radically theological
and one radically antitheological-existentialist, which have given
up man's essence over against existence—the former as a result of
the fall, the latter through identification of essential man and existing man—with the consequence that a political utopia and therefore
norms of political actions generally have become impossible. This is
the great danger, I feel, of both currents, politically speaking. If it
is impossible to derive norms from the essence of man then they
can only come, as Barth contends, from an pure theology of revelation.

Closely related to the existentialists and yet distinct from them
are the pragmatists, and I would like to report something about
them from my American experience. For this group also there are
no norms; norms are the pragmatic tools that we utilize at every
moment; when they are no longer usable, they are promptly dis-
carded. A debate often arose between these pragmatists and myself
or other advocates of a critical humanism. The results of these
debates showed clearly that if the American pragmatists were

consistent, they would be just as lacking in norms, ethical and political (in this case), as the existentialists are—and as the Nazis, who ultimately identified the norm with a biological reality, the nation, transcendent critical norms having disappeared. But this does not happen in America. Why not? Once I had a debate with John Dewey—a champion of humanism against every form of totalitarianism—in which I asked him: "How can you counter the criticism that you reputedly have no norms, against Nazism, for example? How can you reconcile your championing of humanism against every form of totalitarianism with your doctrine of pragmatic instrumentalism? Where is the criterion?" He was unable to reply and basically agreed when I reminded him that these norms derive from the still unbroken tradition of Anglo-Saxon humanism. In other words, the happy inconsistency of the Anglo-Saxons has saved them from the European fate. Had it not been so, there would have been a similar destruction of norms, of essence, and therefore of authentic utopian invention. So much for the two types that eliminate essence and thereby render utopia impossible.

Over against them are two other currents of thought which acknowledge the possibility of an intra-historical restoration. The first is characterized by a radical change from consummate sinfulness, or the lowest point, to a new high point. It is very interesting that the Christian and the humanist-secularist lines of thought converge here. In Christianity there is the idea of the Millennium, one of the most fateful and momentous ideas of Christian history, the idea from which probably all modern Western utopias ultimately derive. What does this idea mean? The "thousand years" is naturally a symbolic number; they lie, however, before the final end, that is, within history, and they signify that at some point in history human expectation will be given to us. With this expectation Christian sects throughout their history have continued to attack the Augustinian position, which is very similar to the Barthian insofar as the last age no longer lies before us but, as Augustine says, the "thousand years" are the present rule of the church. Christian sects from the Montanists to radical communism, however, form an unbroken movement of groups that believe there is a *dialectic* that makes the great reversal inevitable once the deepest No has been reached consummate sinfulness; industrial class

society); then, at that moment, something will be actualized within history. In this dialectical interpretation—revolutionary-dialectical it should be called—dialectic is the logical expression for historical destiny. It is historical destiny that leads to the greatest depth of dehumanization and from this depth brings about the resurrection, namely, the actualization of man. This is the revolutionary current of thought; it characterizes all revolutions of the Western world. Among these are the inner-churchly revolutions (which were in part very radical, such as monasticism, for example, and later, Protestantism and the radical sects of the Reformation period) and the secular revolutions (for example, the revolutions of bourgeois society against feudalism in the nineteenth and twentieth centuries [sic]).[1] Both types were based on the belief that the essence of man can be restored within history through a historical destiny, namely, through the antithesis of the uttermost depth and the highest height. This belief accounts for the extraordinary revolutionary tension of these men.

Then there is a second current, that of the moderate utopia or the *utopia of the idea of progress* of bourgeois society. Generally speaking, the new society that arises from the revolutionary impetus of the idea of utopia no longer knows what to do with this idea once the revolution has triumphed. This was certainly true of the bourgeois revolutions of eighteenth and nineteenth century Europe. Everything had been won, bourgeois society had established itself in power, the principles that had represented radicalism during the course of the struggle against feudalism were now put into practice. Then there ensued—since the scheme to which one owes one's existence is not easily abandoned—the gradualist utopia, the utopia of the idea of progress, where slowly, step by step, an advance is made. Sometimes this advance is thought eventually to reach its goal; sometimes not, as in the Neo-Kantian school. This utopia has been quite dangerous in recent decades precisely because it is so moderate and so deeply rooted in the practice of all of us.

All of you are here only because you have the utopian hope that you will be able, at least in some way, to confirm and advance your present thinking. This involves a kind of practical faith in prog-

---

[1] Tillich probably means to say "eighteenth and nineteenth centuries" here. See next paragraph. (Tr.)

ress. This practical faith in progress may result in the formulation of a universal law of progress which pervades all of history and for which the American slogan "better and better" is the most graphic expression. Progress is a moderated utopia that is no longer sure of itself but nevertheless determined not to give up. This moderation is particularly dangerous, however, for it is in a special way prone to obscure the difference between what man essentially is and what he is in existence, and thus to produce a utopianism that is remote from the real world. The result may be expressed in a quotation from Goethe: "Him who strives with ceaseless effort, we can surely save." Salvation is accordingly the result of striving and effort. Goethe himself was too great to intend this meaning, but his words could be interpreted in this sense. In America this conception is widely held. It finds expression, among other places, in the English version of the angels' anthem at the birth of Christ. The biblical text reads, "good will to men," which is rendered, "to men of good will." This conception is one of the most fantastic utopias I have ever encountered. Ever again a gain, one meets this belief that sooner or later many men of good will—and naturally we include ourselves among them—will obtain permanent control of things and then peace on earth will be realized. What the consequences of this belief have been, and to what terrible disillusionment it has led, I shall say more about in my next lecture. I can assure you, however, that in America's academic institutions a wave of what the Americans call "cynicism" is rising today, a kind of bored, supercilious indifference to all questions of content and all norms. I say this in order to make fully clear the significance of this progressivist utopia.

2. HISTORICAL AND UNHISTORICAL THINKING

The development of our exposition thus far has been as follows: The problem of utopia must first of all be dealt with by way of an analysis of man's being. Man, as we saw, is that being who has possibility; from possibility comes anxiety, and anxiety makes itself felt in two ways. The first is concerned not with the actualizing of what is possible but with the safeguarding of what is given; this is the backward-looking, conservative and, in the case of struggle against progress, reactionary will. The second is concerned with the losing of possibilities, with expectancy, which gives rise to a progressive and, under certain conditions, a revolutionary type of thought and action. On this foundation of a total view of man we then said that the concept of utopia is dependent upon a distinction between what man essentially should and could be and what he existentially—that is, actually—is. This contrast is revealed, as we saw, in man's projection of his true being in an ideal time of the past, in a mythical past described as a paradise, an angelic existence, a golden age, as the first stage of an evolutionary development, as an age of innocence, and so on. This essential image, which man forms of himself and projects into the past, becomes the criterion that he applies to the reality in which he stands and out of which he creates an ideal image of what he could be because of what he has been at one time. I pointed to the cognate relation of the German words *Wesen* (essence) and *gewesen* (been) and showed how man's essence comes to be viewed as that which has been but now no longer is. We considered various ideal structures and distinguished two groups —those that say Yes and those that say No to utopia. Among the latter we distinguished the existentialists and the pessimistic form of Protestant Christianity, and in a somewhat paradoxical way we compared on this point the typical radical Protestant Karl Barth with the typical radical existentialist Sartre. In contrast to these, we distinguished the two types of utopia—first, the revolutionary type, which rejects a condition of total corruption and, with revolutionary expectancy, looks for a state of perfection to be born out of it; and second, the stance of the victorious revolution, which has no further need of radical change but on the basis of its victory seeks to attain the ideal through gradual progress. These observations led us immediately to the threshold of today's topic, the question of the meaning of history in relation to the concept of utopia.

Today's lecture has as its subject "Historical and Unhistorical Thinking and the Function of Utopia." Let me first express a few ideas about unhistorical thinking; that is, about an understanding of history which is born not from history but from something other than history and which consequently grants history no independent standing, no autonomy, but makes it dependent on something else and thus dissolves it. In order to understand the

diametrically opposed concepts of unhistorical and historical thinking, we must plunge again into the human situation, which in this
case is shared by all that exists. By the human situation we mean
man's subjection to the so-called categories, the forms in which we
perceive and think and which, as space and time, at every moment
play a decisive role for all existence and therefore have always
stood in the center of philosophical thought.

The question is: Which category, space or time, is dominant and
decisive in a particular way of life? There are ways of life determined by space and ways of life determined by time, and the question of historical and unhistorical thinking is: How are they related
to one another? For which of the two can or must we take a stand?
Unhistorical thinking is a type of thinking in which space is superior
to time, and time is subordinated to, and incorporated into, space.
You all know that in modern physics time, represented by the symbol "t," has become one of the four dimensions of space. This is one
of the most interesting symbols for the subordination of time to
space.

What are the world-views in which space is set over time? I should
like to distinguish two or, rather, three. The first goes beyond nature
to the ground of being and from there subjects time to space; it is
the classical mysticism of India and Europe. In *classical mysticism*
true reality is what is dissociated from the temporal flux, and everything that is real proceeds from this ground of pure being, the
"abyss" of being—from the divine ground. It may be useful here to
interpret the symbol "ground." The word "ground," which is often
connected with "abyss" because it is indeed an unfathomable ground
in which being rests, is a spatial metaphor; and a philosophy that
speaks of "ground" and "abyss" is by that very fact characterized
as a philosophy (and a religion) in which space—not actual space,
not our space, but rather the spatial as such—contributes the highest
symbol. This is characteristic of mysticism. In mysticism it is the
dimension of depth from which everything is understood, in which
everything is submerged, and out of which everything arises. Time,
as it were, is a ripple on the surface of this ocean, and thus this conception of the world is essentially unhistorical. The interesting thing
is that we are confronted here with a conception of the world in
which history means nothing. We find this typically in India, which

has no recollection of history, no chronicles, no historical memory, and which is always at every moment directly in contact with the ground of being, with Brahman, pure being which brings forth from itself and receives back into itself all concrete forms. We find the same conception in the West in Neoplatonism, where the individual soul and the return of the individual are decisive, and where history means nothing because the individual under every historical condition is equally distant from the "One" from whom he has fallen away and to whom he longs to return. It is a purely vertical conception—the horizontal is without any significance.

This is not relevant in itself, but what is relevant to our theme is that although this type of thinking is fundamentally unhistorical, it still does not escape the essence of man: his bondage to time, his quest of the future, his anxiety about the past and the future. This is apparent, for example, in the fact that there is in India a philosophy of history that is ultimately dependent on the doctrine of Brahman, the principle of all being which is at the same time the innermost part of every individual soul and of every particular thing, producing a rhythm, a rhythm of inhaling and exhaling. When Brahman exhales, a world comes into being; when he inhales, this world perishes. I say "Brahman," not "Brahma," not a god, Brahma, who is himself only a god, who is inhaled and exhaled like all gods, for in India the gods are no more than men, but Brahman is the Original Principle, the Abyss of Being itself, the One. When it unfolds itself in the metaphor of exhaling, the empirical world comes into being, and when it contracts itself in the metaphor of inhaling, the empirical world ceases to be. In this way world-periods arise, periods of coming into existence and periods of passing out of existence. In these cosmic cycles Indian thought, despite its unhistorical character, has paid its tribute to utopian thinking, which it could not wholly avoid, since it lies in man's essence. The idea is quite similar to the Stoic conception, as we shall presently see. Immediately after the exhalation, after the moment in which the world begins, there is a period of the unity of all essences, a period of peace, of growth, of creativity, of spirituality—a period characterized by terms like "golden age" or "paradise." As in all these utopias, one lives now in the last period. Little by little the characteristics of the first period have been lost. Now not only mankind but also nature has become diseased, and there comes a moment when the whole will perish. Various theories are advanced for this, but they all agree that the depth of corruption is the end of a cosmic cycle, which is followed by a new one. I repeat: the important thing about this is that it has shown the inevitability of utopian thinking in these modes of thought even on Indian soil, the soil of unhistorical mysticism. It is, should we wish so to formulate it, a backward-looking utopia, a utopia that lies in the past. History is not progress but deterioration, decay, corruption, disintegration—nothing but negative terms. Utopia lies in the past and not in the future. If you consider that this is and was the feeling for life not only of the great ascetic, mystically oriented religions but also of classical Hellenism, insofar as it is represented by the Stoics and others, it becomes immediately clear how extraordinary it is that our culture has taken the idea of progress for granted; and that it was shaken by possibly the greatest historical convulsions history has ever seen, namely, those of the twentieth century.

The second form of unhistorical thinking is *naturalism*. While the first makes supernature, so to speak or, rather, the ground of nature, the basis of nonhistorical thinking, the second makes the eternal return as one observes it in nature (or believes he can) the foundation for denying all significance to history. The symbol that is decisive for understanding the world and its events is found in Greek philosophy—and not only for the Stoics. It is the circle. The circle is a spatial symbol; unlike time, it does not go forward but turns back upon itself. In other words, even in the naturalistic thought of Greece time is subordinated to space. The Stoic doctrine of the world-conflagration is quite similar to the doctrine of the inhalation of Brahman: After an indefinitely long, incalculable period the world—that is, this order of things (the cosmos, for "cosmos" means "order")—ends, and another order of things follows. This period is bounded by two world-conflagrations: the fire, however, should not be taken in a physical sense but as a symbol for the self-consuming power of being. What has always made fire a symbol in philosophy is that in its self-consuming it rises to consummation and expends itself at the same time. These world-conflagrations delimit a world-period which passes through succeeding stages that are frequently designated by metals—gold, silver, iron, clay—which likewise are not to be taken physically but symbolically. Here, too, the present stage is the last one. It is interesting that at the height of modern culture, on one of the highest peaks of imagination and thought, Nietzsche has repeated these Stoic ideas and interpreted the doctrine of the eternal return as his greatest revelation, which came to him close by that stone in Sils-Maria where I have often sat reverently, and which for him is a conception of the world that enables him absolutely to contradict the whole Christian world-view.

In the face of this line of thought we must pose the question: How can utopia arise here? And yet it does arise in both cases. In Stoicism, just as in India, it is a backward-looking utopia; it is the Golden Age that is past and never returns, for after the world-conflagration we are not there to experience anything—it is of course not the same history. From that derives the tragic character of the world-view of late antiquity, of which stoicism is the perfect manifestation following the great expression that the tragedians had given it in the classical period. It is a world-view according to which nothing redemptive can occur in history: history goes forward, but continues to deteriorate, and only the solitary, courageous Stoic rises above the events of the world and unites with eternal reason, the divine Logos, which is exalted over all the world. It is a tragico-heroic world-view like the entire Greek world-view and, just as in India, its utopia is backward-looking. But perhaps still more interesting, or at least more noteworthy, is the solution Nietzsche attempted, namely, to combine both the Greek idea of eternal circularity, which implies a tragic dominance of space over time, and a tremendously dynamic forward thrust of thinking and feeling which empowers him in a fully utopian manner to foresee and anticipate the coming of the Great Noonday, the coming of *the* Man who follows upon man and who is only ostensibly called man. That is the meaning of the Superman: a new self-realization of life which surpasses everything that has existed up until now. Consider this extraordinary tension—which can be labeled contradiction in a logical analysis of Nietzsche but which has far outgrown every such paltry analysis because in reality it grasps human elements in symbols and, in an unrehearsed language, half-poetic, half-philosophical, gives such expression that these symbols are continuously effective and have created history. This cannot always be said of the non-contradictory systems of professors of philosophy.

The third form of unhistorical thinking is *existentialism*, about which I have spoken in another place and which I take very much more seriously than those who identify it with a few paradoxical ideas of the French existentialist Jean-Paul Sartre. In existentialism there is neither a circle nor a forward-pressing line, but a point, and this point is what the existentialists call freedom. The individual, however, who in absolute solitariness faces his death, who is thrown back upon himself and from there expands his point into a limited circle, his totality, and takes his stand in this experience, has no essential relation to history. The free individual in existential philosophy keeps going (*geht*) just up to his death, but history goes on beyond his death. Because he goes (*geht*) only up to his death and then looks back upon himself and thus experiences himself as a whole, he is essentially unhistorical and extrahistorical. Interestingly enough, this fact finds especially clear expression in a concept of Heidegger's which ostensibly demonstrates the opposite, namely, the concept of historicity. Heidegger has abstracted man from all real history, has put him on his own feet, thrown him into his isolation, and out of this entire story he has produced one abstract concept, namely that of historicity, or "the ability–to-have-history." This is what makes man, man. But this idea is the very negation of every concrete relation to history.

I would like to make an observation here, however, which must be made parenthetically, so to speak, for those who have read Heidegger's latest writings; for here suddenly something else emerges. Heidegger gains a relation to history, first of all to the history of philosophy, and it may be that one day he will go further. He now speaks of language as "the house of being." But language after all has a history, and if being reveals itself in language, history should thereby take on new meaning for him. And perhaps one could elaborate this point so that, just as with other groups, a hidden utopia could be confirmed even among the existentialists, namely, the utopia of the "revelation of pure being," which Heidegger awaits like a prophet who gazes upon a hidden holy mountain. He calls it "being itself" in distinction from all particular beings. From it he expects a revelation. Should it come, the age of metaphysics would be at an end, that is, the age in which man attaches himself to the forms of being instead of to pure being; and should he attach himself to pure being . . . this sentence cannot be carried further at present. This hidden utopia of the existentialists shows how even this radical extrahistorical form of thinking eventually finds its lot bound up with history. I believe that Sartre's participation in the Resistance Movement has somewhat to do with this insofar as he saw that the concept of the absolute freedom of the individual is somehow connected with social and political freedom and that it is impossible to realize one completely without the other. Thus human reality, and in this case the historical situation, has wrenched him loose and into a historical thinking that his principles opposed. He would perhaps answer: "My participation in the Resistance was action, and action is human self-realization; but the particular act itself is not what matters—I could also have done the opposite." But no one would believe that he could have. And if this is true, then an element of historical relatedness is there and perhaps even an element of utopia, namely, the expectation that in the individual, through his struggle for freedom of decision, the system of objectification and authority will one day be overcome.

This brings me to the end of the three types of unhistorical thinking. I repeat: my effort has been to show that each of them contains a utopian element that cannot be denied, not even by those who think unhistorically.

In contrast to these are the types of thinking in which history comes to be understood from history itself and not from what underlies nature or from the repetitive natural process or from the isolated individual. If historical thinking is to be possible, then time must have triumphed over space, and this is the case in the historical concept of time. Historical time is time that runs ahead—inescapable, irreversible, nonrepeatable—time that moves toward what is new. Heidegger has here pointed to the deep meaning implicit in the German word *zeitigen* (to ripen, to mature), which is derived from *Zeit* (time) and means that time creates the new out of itself: the new "ripens." It is interesting to compare a similar derivation in English, the derivation of "timing" (which means watching for the right moment) from "time." But at the right moment everything is given; nothing new is created. And this is the difference between a world-view that in the last analysis is controlled by technical reason, which consequently does the technically right thing at the right time, and a romantic world-view that would like to see the creative thing in every moment of time. This does not mean that I deprecate the one against the other, although I would like to emphasize the concept of "ripening" (*Zeitigen*) which is connected with the concept of the new and which acquired paramount significance for the philosophy of history.

The victory of time over space is not the victory of abstract concepts in philosophy but a victory within history. The victory of time is fundamentally and above all a victory over polytheism and all its secular forms, the most important and devastating of which is nationalism. Polytheism, whether in its religious form or in its secular form (that is, nationalism), has a character that clearly displays the marks of the preponderance of space over time. Polytheism is surely not the acceptance of many gods in contrast to one God—it is the absolutizing of one space among other spaces. The god who rules this space, this sphere of value, is the absolute god; but the other gods make the same claim, and this is the devastating, disruptive, and demonically destructive side of polytheism. Plurality, like singularity, is in itself a matter of indifference. To speak of God is not to pose a riddle of numbers—to inquire into the idea of God is to play no numbers game; on the contrary, what is involved is the question of space and time; that is, whether a limited space is worthy of making an absolute claim. Is Athena so exalted as to exclude Mars? May Zeus exclude Aphrodite? May Apollo—to cite the outstanding Greek example—exclude Dionysus? This is polytheism, the experience of being, encounter with being, symbolized by these gods, whose reality I have never doubted. This encounter with being in these powers of being, in these gods, is fatal if it is an encounter with spaces that make absolute claims one against the other. Now let us apply this principle to secularized polytheism, to nationalism, for example, or to family relations, which have the same character. There is an absolutism of the family which even calls itself altruistic but which is nothing other than a polytheistic worship of space, namely, the space of this family. This is ominous, although not in the measure in which nationalism is. It is a modern form of polytheism against which we have to fight just as the ancient prophets had to fight against the ancient polytheism. We must take the side of time against space.

What happens when we do this? A remarkable duality makes its appearance. On the one hand, all individual spaces are now joined together; they lose their independent significance and are swallowed up in a temporal process that is equally valid for them all. On the other hand, a universal struggle takes place among the various principles, one that pervades all spaces and from which history (and with it, expectation and utopia) gains its dynamism, its immense interest, its passion, and its real significance. Let me illustrate this by giving several examples.

At an early period in the history of religion we find a historical thinking that is characterized by the joining together of all spaces and their permeation by a universal struggle—the struggle of two principles that are not spatially bound but are the same everywhere. This phenomenon first appears in ancient Persia in the religion of Zoroaster (or Zarathustra, both names are attested), in which the good and the evil principles engage in a cosmic struggle. At the end a situation arises in which one side overcomes the other, what is called dark or evil, Ahriman, is overcome by the side of light or good, Ormazd, the god of light. The negative elements are being destroyed, the utopia becomes a reality and the demonic is exorcised. For how long? The Persian religion does not know, and this is very important; for it shows that there may still persist in it a last vestige of cyclical thinking which has not yet been fully overcome. In any case, in the history of religion this is the first known instance of a religion giving rise to cosmic, world-historical thinking. For us it is important because it influenced the later stages of Israelite thought and provided the basis for certain New Testament concepts. The prophets' struggle for Yahweh against polytheism in Israel is likewise a struggle against these same hostile principles, which frequently come to be symbolized by the nation. As a nation Israel, too, stands constantly under judgment because it seeks to absolutize itself as nation, instead of being community of God. We find the same idea again in the church; Christ and Antichrist—the church of Christ and the community of Antichrist—which fight with each other and come to be identified with various empirical realities, with the empirical church occasionally on one side, the state or the political powers on the other. Here, too, the temporal process is seen as one: one struggle and one end, the thousand-year reign—that is, that which is beyond all history.

The same idea is found in the revolutionary middle class of the eighteenth century where from sectarian movements the idea arises that reason and unreason struggle with each other in world history, that reason gradually becomes victorious, that the Age of Reason has dawned, and that consequently all people through education and political revolution will be brought to reason. Utopia lies before us in the revolution in which the remaining elements of oppressive authoritarian unreason are to be removed and democracy is to be actualized as a system involving the reason of every individual.

The proletarian movements belong to the same line of historical thinking, for there, too, we discover a unity that extends over the whole world (for example, the Communist Manifesto, a summons to the proletariat of all lands); and, on the other hand, we find the struggle of the classes which makes history, and the utopia of the classless society which lies before us.

In all these conceptions space has ceased to play a role, time means everything. Nevertheless, man still lives in space, and thus a problem arises which I would like only to suggest here but which has come to have vast historical significance. It was surely not a nonspatial kingdom that Israel expected but Palestine, Mount Zion, to which all nations will come. We have seen the significance of this spatial element in the Zionist movement, in the fulfillment of its longing, and in the enormous problems that issue from it for Jewish self-understanding. All Jews whom I know, who have acknowledged the belief that Israel is the people of time and therefore bound to no space but stand in all spaces without space, are greatly apprehensive lest a new spatial bondage should arise out of the Zionist movement, a spatial bondage that will then manifest itself as nationalistic, polytheistic, and against which the full power of prophecy will have to be brought to bear. In rebuttal, the Zionists say—this I have learned through the events of the last decade— that a being in time is no being, that in the concept of the present —that is, of real being—space and time are bound up together, that in order to be, I must have not only time but also space, and that consequently the demand for space is just as natural as the demand that a people take time seriously. The tension between these two elements has always been, and is today more than ever, *the* problem of Judaism and also of Christianity.

With these remarks I come to Rome. There we have not only the idea of temporal progression but also the sacred center of space, from which the kingdom of God, insofar as it is represented in the church, shines forth, is directed, and finds its place. Here again it was the Protestant protest that negated this spatial bondage and created nonspatial groups in all lands, who rebeled against space and with prophetic pathos submitted themselves to time—but who in the historical actualization felt yet again the need to find a space. And this appears to me to be the problem of the ecumenical movement: that—perchance at Geneva or at some other place—a space will be established again, not because the ground is sacred but because a center then becomes possible; and that then once again protest will erupt against this unity of Protestantism.

In order to emphasize the importance of the problem of space, I need only remind you that two great civilizations, the Greek and the Chinese, have called their territories "Lands of the Middle." The absolute significance of Greek culture is described spatially in the first chapters of Aristotle's *Politics* where he points out that in the four cardinal directions barbarians are found or climatic conditions make it impossible for a culture to flourish. Thus, Greece is the civilized center. And similarly, China is the "Middle Kingdom." There is a wonderful and profoundly metaphysical poem in the form of a soliloquy of the Chinese emperor in which he explains how he feels himself to be the center of all being—not as an individual but as the locus of the center.

This is the problem of space and time. Space is rejected, but it cannot be entirely rejected, not even in Israel, not even in the church and, as we see today, not even in the proletariat. There, too, at least in one form of the proletarian revolution, a spatial center has been formed—Moscow—which has exactly the same function as the other spaces, namely, to impede the Protestant protest from which this movement originally arose and to "normalize" it within an ultimate spatial bondage.

I come, in closing, to a few observations concerning the character

of the time that I have described as "historical time." Historical
time is a unity in precisely the sense in which we spoke of space as
a unity, and it has a center, just as we spoke of the center of space.
But this "time" that has a center is now something utterly different
from space that has a center. The center of time is that locus where
the meaning of the temporal process has been actualized objectively
for a moment and in such a way that it not only gives meaning to
the whole but also determines backward, the beginning; and forward, the end. Thus from this center arise backward- and forward-
looking utopias. Let me make this clear by examples. Consider
Israel. The center of its history is undoubtedly the exodus from
Egypt—the entire Judaic cultus is centered on this event—and from
it history gains its meaning. It is the moment in which Israel is separated from an alien space and has to seek its own space. From that
point the beginning is identified, namely, in Abraham, the symbolic
first personality in whom the same thing has already happened.
Abraham is characterized as he who was called out of a closed cultic
space into something spatially undefined, "a land that I will show
you"—a floating concept that shows how the spatial is replaced by
the temporal, even though the latter finds a space again. The end,
too, is identified from that point, as the moment in which all peoples
are loosed from their national bonds and come to the place where
the no-longer-spatial God nevertheless has a space, namely Mount
Zion, to which all peoples return and where the King of Peace reigns
—a plenitude of symbols in which the spatial, despite its in-
escapability, has still not yet overcome the absolute dominance of
the temporal.

It is exactly the same with Rome. In Rome the center was for a
time the beginning of the Republic, the abolition of the kingship;
later, the center was the Augustan *Pax Romana,* the origin, as before, was the founding of Rome, with the end being the situation
foreseen by the Stoics, in which Roman law rules all lands and
creates not only outward but also inward justice. (As you know, it
was the Stoic emperors who accomplished the emancipation of
women, foreigners, and, eventually, slaves.)

We could give many additional examples. Every people has a
center that serves to orient its philosophy of history and posits its
beginning and its end. This is true also of Christianity where the

center is unquestionably given in the appearance of the Christ, and where the beginning is a double one, at one time the mythical moment of the fall, from which history arises, and at another, Abraham. The future is also double—the millennial state is contrasted with the final end, the world-conflagration and the eternal establishment of the kingdom of God. Here you have a structuring of history which proceeds from the center and which is also capable of detailed elaboration.

The new comes to birth in history. What is the new? In one respect it is the restoration of the old—not simply a restoration, however, but the elevation of the old to something new, to a new creation; this is the most profound basis of every utopia. In modern process-philosophy, the philosophy of becoming, the concept of the new has acquired a meaning that goes far beyond what I have just said. Men such as Bergson and Whitehead, and before them Schelling, have attempted to relate natural time with its infinite continuation to historical time with its progression from one new event to another, but they have done it without positing a beginning, a middle, or an end. This brings us to the question: What about the problem of utopia? The answer can only be that here utopia has been lost. In Bergson we have no utopia, we have the *élan vital,* the dynamic, creative, and continuing life-force. Bergson has asserted even of God, who for him is the ground of the life-process, that he can be identified only in relation to the past, for in relation to the future God himself is open and does not know, so to speak, what the future will be. In Whitehead we have the same idea: a process in which infinite possibilities always come to be realized in new ways; and in which the vital process therefore continues infinitely without the idea of a fall or of a utopia, without past or future confronting the present. The sole form in which something ultimate is found in Whitehead is his idea that all creativity works, so to speak, for Eternity, is there preserved, and becomes an enrichment of the divine over and beyond what was there in the divine. This, however, is without limit; it can go on and on, and allows of no utopia. The same holds true for Bergson in whom the retention of what is now at hand plays a similar role.

With this I am at the end of the discussion of the various attitudes toward utopia. Within these diverse philosophical currents it was only in the last one that we found a world-view in which utopia was reduced to a point where nothing remains of it besides the eternal affirmation of whatever is valuable in history. In neither case is there any progress in the proper sense of the term. Even in pragmatist philosophy the progress involved in growth is an idea that is not carried through to a perfect maturing in the utopian sense. The philosophy of becoming knows that all growth also involves loss. Is it a more realistic view than the many utopian conceptions of the world?

3. RELIGIOUS AND SECULAR UTOPIAS

In the first part of this lecture series we spoke about man and utopia and in the second part about history and utopia. We dealt with the different interpretations of history and saw that in every interpretation utopian elements are present because it belongs to man's essence to project something utopian beyond himself. We also saw that among all interpretations of history the prophetic interpretation is the one that lies nearest to utopian thinking. Thus far, however, we have not spoken in any way about the material aspects of utopia, namely, what is meant by utopia and what thought it expresses.

We have not even spoken of the origin of the word "utopia." To all who know Greek it is obvious that the English word comes from the two Greek words οὐ (no) and τόπος (place)—*that which has no place,* that for which there is not yet or is no longer a place in reality, which can nowhere be found even though one go to the most remote islands. Should one seek "the isles of the blest," to use the fairytale style of some utopias, one would not find them; these utopias have no place. The word "utopia" has become known through the *Utopia* of Thomas More, the English chancellor and philosopher, and ever since it has been a term of abuse or of praise; it is more abusive than laudatory at present. If something has no place it has no presence, for "presence" is the point where space and time are one. Only that which has space, only that which has a place, is in truth present. The word "presence" (*Gegenwart*), that which "stands over against" (*gegenübersteht*), expresses clearly this union of space and time. When we speak of utopia, therefore, we speak of something that is already characterized by the name itself as having no space and no time, no presence, but as that which comes out of the past as recollection and is an anticipation of what may come in the future.

And now we ask for the first time in this series: What are the contents of the utopian consciousness? Are there definite forms of utopian consciousness, are there specific contents, distinct types? The answer is that there are; and I would like to speak about some of these forms and their historical meaning. The principle of all utopias is the *negation of the negative*—the representation of a condition as once present or once again to be present in which the negative side of existence is negated, in which this negative side was not yet real or is no longer real. This presupposes that our present condition, which has a locus, a *tópos,* the one in which we live, is determined by negativities, by forms of nonbeing. Precisely this is the proper starting-point for approaching the problem of utopia. Here we can discover what fundamental types of utopia are conceivable and have become actual.

There are, we might say, two fundamental negative experiences that determine the present, or actual existence, which we commonly call historical time. They are *finitude,* the mixture of being and nonbeing, and *estrangement,* the contradiction between what we essentially are and what we actually are. Estrangement is experienced in two ways, as guilt and as meaninglessness. These negative elements are present in the experience of every one of us at every moment. They have their locus, they are not utopian but are real and appear to banish every utopia into the land of fanciful wishes. These finite states do not appear separately but almost always in unified images.

When the myth of paradise is recounted, for instance, whether in biblical or nonbiblical form, its content is the following: In paradise, or the golden age, in the primal condition or whatever it may be called, there is no suffering. For suffering is the finitude that we experience as fated and which derives from other finite things or from the boundaries that constitute our finitude. And there is no death, for death is the absolute limit, the total expression of finitude. Finitude is sublated (*aufgehoben*). There is no myth, however, in which paradise, the original condition, is represented in such a way that man stands naturally beyond finitude. Man is not freed from finitude by nature but by virtue of his participation in a life that is intrinsically eternal and which is commonly symbolized as the life of the gods. In paradise, moreover, there is no separation of man and nature; man lives in such a unity with nature that he enters into its secrets and is accordingly able to give names to animals and plants. This is a remarkable and intriguing myth, and it signifies two things. It means, first, that man is joined with nature in such a way that he has knowledge of it, for to know the name of a thing is to know its essence—at least that is what it meant in a time when words were still expressions of reality and not merely a means of communication. But the word is at the same time magic power— he who knows the name has power over that whose name he knows. But in paradise and the Golden Age there is also no separation of man and man—the community is united. All this is possible because in paradise there is no separation from the ground of creation, from the creative ground, because the world and man are still united with the ground, not yet having broken away from it. Or, as it could be said in another terminology, they are still innocent, not yet having undergone estrangement from the ground from which they come. Doubt, therefore, does not exist in paradise, in the primordial state of things, in the golden age, for doubt presupposes, of course, that a separation has taken place. Nor has meaninglessness been experienced, for meaninglessness presupposes that the ground of meaning is no longer present. My intention here has been to show that in the myth of the primal state, that is, in the backward-looking utopia, all forms of negativity have not yet appeared. And in the same manner I shall interpret the forward-looking utopia, the myth of the final state of things as opposed to the original one, as in all respects the conquest of finitude.

Let me give a few examples of these symbols of utopia, make their meaning intelligible insofar as possible, attempt to free them from certain superficial conceptions, and thereby give an account of one of the greatest and most momentous forces in the life-process of the individual and of peoples. I begin with the *utopia of the conquest of death,* that reality in which finitude is absolutely manifest. We must ever look more deeply into the myths of immortality, for the utopia of exemption from death in the beginning, and that of the overcoming of death in the end are, in this respect, more profound than much philosophical talk about the immortality of the soul, since they assert nothing of this kind but rather—in the words of the Old Testament account—that we are taken from dust and to dust we return, that it belongs to man's essence to be finite, that is, to be mortal. The paradise story accordingly says nothing about a natural immortality. Nearly all myths have the same character. In the paradise story the life that conquers death is derived from eating the divine food from the tree of life, from the very food that makes the gods immortal—a symbol for a kind of being which belongs to the ground of being, to being itself which stands beyond time. Only he who partakes of the divine food is immortal, and Adam and Eve are driven out of paradise because the gods do not wish that, having acquired knowledge (that is, magic power over the good and evil forces of reality), they should now also participate in the eternity of the divine being. To understand this idea is to understand what the ancient church did when it designated the Lord's Supper the *pharmakon athanasias,* the "medicine of immortality." The idea becomes fully clear in connection with this interpretation of the paradise story. The eating of the new being, of the new reality of the divine body of the Christ (in the mystical sense, of course), is exactly the same as what in paradise was the eating of the tree of life. What was lost in paradise is recovered in the Lord's Supper—but only fragmentarily, because every mortal body has attained an independence that makes it impossible for it to become immortal through the Lord's Supper. But by means of the Lord's Supper another immortal body is born—that is, participation in the divine being begins to restore the paradise of the past and thus to overcome natural finitude and mortality. We should take these ideas much more seriously than we do, because that would provide a quite different understanding of the myth of immortality. Not natural immortality but lost and restored participation in the Eternal— this is the doctrine that might be developed from this idea. In the Platonic school another conception of immortality evolved which is already problematic in Plato himself. Socrates in the *Phaedo* treats the proofs for the immortality of the soul half-seriously, half-ironically. The certainty he has is not based on these proofs but on the possibility of affirming his true being, of preserving inner freedom in the face of the necessity of having to die. Neither is there to be found here, as in many modern religious philosophies, and even in ancient ones, the idea that an indestructible substance can be rationally demonstrated; but in Plato there is still the elemental experience, namely, that in Socrates is embodied a reality, a courage, a self-affirmation which is not the courage to continue forever but the courage to assert the true essence, the essence of the *logikon,* as essential and meaningful. Here again we should clearly see that the notion of the simple continuation of an immortal substance is something that cannot be derived even from Plato and which in any case cannot be derived from Christianity.

The notion of immortality as continuation, as a natural endowment of man, is a notion that belongs, especially in the religious culture of America today, to one of the most important remnants of the great religious tradition. It is not shocking in America to call in question the idea of God—that is tolerated if necessary—but to call in question the notion of immortality, which has acquired a kind of Christian standing as a rationalized form of Platonism, strikes at the root of faith. The paradox—the enormity of the idea—that the finite can participate in the Eternal has been lost, and has been replaced by a conception that has deep roots and is affirmed with strong personal commitment. This is the conception of an individual continuation beyond death in forms not very different from those of life. Let us suppose that continuation beyond our death could be conceived, as in anthroposophic or occult myths. The problem of finitude would still not be solved. Finitude would merely have become prolonged in duration.

One of the consequences of this notion of immortal continuation struck me in a discussion I had with a very typical spokesman of this kind of American theology where the utopia developed by this theologian looked somewhat like this: of course we survive as responsible personalities and as individuals; but though we, happily, are released from the body and also from nature, the individual immortal soul continues to perfect itself and others, just as it had done previously in a good Christian congregation, only without the hindrances that still obtain here. It was a simple extension into the infinite of the Puritan ethic of work and self-conquest, which was identified with eternity and with the overcoming of death. In response I had to observe that this is not Christian, for in Christianity there is the idea of the resurrection, which includes the body, and of the participation of the universe (including nature) in the final consummation. In other words, this utopia is a clear projection of an image of perfected man, but man without body, without nature —the pure representative of a Puritan ethos.

The utopia of immortality takes another form in the Enlightenment. At its finest it is expressed by Lessing in his *Education of the Human Race,* where the idea of reincarnation is utilized for very obvious reasons. How can men, who die today or who have died a hundred thousand years ago and are therefore infinitely remote from the essence of man, enter the kingdom of God—the kingdom of Reason? The answer is: they must enter through the history of mankind. And if they have died, they must come back. Thus arises the remarkable phenomenon that at the very summit of the Enlightenment the mythical idea of reincarnation reappears. But here it means that the stages of reincarnation signify degrees of maturation which lead ultimately to a kingdom of Reason. If such ideas as reincarnation are found in the West in a man like Lessing and at the same time in Buddhist myth as well, then you can conclude from that in what diverse forms one and the same utopia may be encountered. Reincarnation for Buddhism is the return of man in a new body, for example, in an animal body. This is the "great curse" from which one must be delivered, and utopia here is the end of this process. For the enlightened Westerner the same idea is reversed from this negative into the absolutely positive—the goal becomes a kingdom of Reason in which every individual has attained maturity.

Compare with this the Christian utopia of immortality which is expressed, for instance, in the Pauline saying that in the end God will be all for all or all in all, and that consequently the universe is included; it is reunited with the Ground from which it came, hence personality, corporeality, community, nature—every empirical reality—are gathered together again in this unity.

We come now to another form of utopia, the *utopia of overcoming estrangement.* Estrangement means first of all the estrangement of man from nature. This is something we all suffer; we have a longing for nature, but we know that nature continues to be alien. Even though as biologists we know a tree minutely, even though we know everything about it that science can tell, this tree still, in

its growth and dying, remains strange to us. What it is for itself we
do not know. We are able to analyze it as an object, but its nature
is a mystery, and it remains a mystery. It is estrangement from
nature which leads to the hostility of nature—consider the hostility
between serpent and man in the paradise myth, which has its beginning in the very moment of temptation; and estrangement is believed to be overcome in two possible ways, through religion and
through technology. An essential element of all utopias is the
miracle of renewal, of new being, of rebirth—Isaiah depicts it as
peace within nature, peace between man and nature and between
nature and nature; even in fables it echoes everywhere. But it is
often thought to be not only a miracle of a magical kind but also
something metaphorically called miracle, the miracle of technology.
This is the background of the *technological utopia*. The true meaning of the technological utopia is not that we can make better tools
—this is a pleasant consequence that can also be unpleasant; but its
true meaning is that we in this way appropriate nature to ourselves
in a form that overcomes estrangement. This appropriation, however, is at the same time also an intensification of estrangement, for
in appropriating nature we transform it, make it into an object, a
tool, a means, and subordinate it to ourselves. Passion for the technological utopia can perhaps no longer be understood in Europe
today, but I shall never forget one of the Chicago theologians whom
I visited shortly after my arrival in America asking me as he wel-
comed me into his study, "Do you know what the kingdom of God
is?" I stammered something, and he then led me to his desk, snapped
on his desk lamp and said, "This is the kingdom of God"—meaning,
of course, the technology making possible man's appropriation of
nature. Only when one has seen and understood that, only when
this faith and its passion are known, can one understand what the
breakdown of this utopia meant in the moment of its culmination.
I cannot say how widely it is known that immediately after the first
three atom bombs were dropped there arose such a forceful reaction
among the leading atomic physicists that it could be said the technological utopia today in the leading circles of physicists has collapsed. The possibility of uniting again with nature and of
establishing the kingdom of God by this means has broken down.
In Thomas More's *Utopia* and in a few other utopias of the same

period of the Renaissance, that is at the beginning of the modern evolution of mathematical natural science, technological domination of the world is the basis for social transformation and for the realization of man's essence; many of the things technology has achieved were anticipated in these utopias. But this does not make them utopias—it makes them prophecies; they are utopias because they conceived the realization of man's essence over against the negativities of nature in the context of technological achievement. The breakdown of this form of utopia therefore has a significance which by no means can be overestimated. When I spoke in another connection (and indeed here, too) of the situation of anxiety in the American world, I had this in mind as one of the motifs bringing about this development. When not only the faith in utopia broke down (which had provided the impetus for "things becoming better and better," as the formula has it, because the technological can indeed always be improved) but also the faith that human self-realization is advanced through the improvement of every kind of technological product, infinitely more collapsed than we here can possibly imagine. In Europe the situation was somewhat different. Characteristically enough, the "reunion with nature" was mainly the concern of poets. Precisely because we do not know what the essence of nature is, since we are estranged from it, we write poetry about our union with it. On our soil this intention was advanced by ideas like the romantic *Natursichtigkeit*. They were enunciated by Klages and the Stefan George School and by the natural scientist Dacqué, and expressed the longing to return to nature but held the way to be mystical, not technical. The fact that this union with the soil has become the symbol of the most frightful kind of political activity constitutes a judgment upon this type of mysticism as well.

One of the most important elements in the *utopia of overcoming estrangement*, which can still be discerned in our church hymns, is the conquest of illness—that is, healing. All that disease produces is overcome, all bodily malfunctions and all diseases that originate outside the body, infections for example. This *utopia of being healed* is one of the greatest forces in the history of mankind. Healing is meant both as reality and as symbol. The meaning of the miracle stories of Jesus is not primarily christological, namely, to show what a divine power he had, but, on the contrary, to show—as the

Gospels make very clear—that the expected utopia, the regeneration of being, of the universe, is about to come. If we would use these healing narratives not so much as miracle stories or as proof for a christological thesis but, rather, to indicate that in every act of healing the coming kingdom of God is already anticipated, its presence already announced, then these stories would gain a vastly new significance for us. It is just in this connection that the problem of healing has become for us, in an altogether different degree from what it had been previously, a metaphysical and universal problem. This reminds us again that *Heil* (salvation) is a cognate of *heilen* (to heal) just as in the romance languages *salvatio* (redemption) means "to make well" *(heilmachen)*, and that both mean "to make whole"; and this refers to both body and soul. The gospels indicate almost everywhere that when the demonic forces that bring about physical destruction are conquered, the New Being makes possible the restoration of the body as well. In this sense healing belongs to utopia, and the symbol of the physician or the healer is an eschatological and hence a utopian symbol of the first rank.

In the context of the naturalistic philosophy of the Enlightenment and its relation to faith in technological progress I was told once by a Marxist friend, a Marxist but in no sense a Stalinist, an important philosopher, that with the coming of a better society the doctrine of finitude would be overcome, for then healing processes would be begun which we today are not at all able to see, and that through them illness would become needless and death indefinitely postponed. The decisive thing was the word "indefinitely." Of course, if death were merely postponed in a limited sense, perhaps about a generation, nothing would be changed fundamentally in an ontology of finitude. Finite is finite, whether the average age is thirty or sixty years. But his thought was that this would be only a beginning, that unlimited healing could be continued and death thereby abolished—through technology, so to speak, instead of through sacraments. It is interesting that from this follows something we ourselves must reflect upon as analogous to the breakdown of the technological utopia: from an economic point of view healing can entail more harm than disease—this I often discovered in conversations with Indians. American aid to India, especially medical aid, means that India's high mortality rate can be reduced; Indian leaders again and again warned us accordingly that incalculable misery would be the result, because the country would not be able to bear the population increase that would ensue. The changing proportion of age groups developing in countries like America is itself a problem that indicates the ambiguity attaching to this purely immanental type of utopia.

I would like to point out in addition, although it is dangerous to do so, that it is an open question whether a purely technological advancement in our ability to heal can be endorsed. The more perceptive psychologists and depth-psychologists know that illness has a positive function and that neurosis, the diminution of the life-basis, can have a creative function precisely through this diminution that the merely healthy may not have. Thus slowly a problem evolves which I only suggest here but which I shall deal with fully in the next lecture—the problem of the relation of the intra-historical to the supra-historical utopia. All the symbols of which I have spoken are valid for both.

These observations, resulting from the analysis of the myth of paradise, lead us to the *social utopia*—to the negation of those evils that come from the social structure. I believe that when I was invited to speak about utopia it was especially these utopias that were primarily meant. But an error is involved here, for the social utopia can never be dealt with in isolation from the other phenomena of estrangement and finitude. If it is, it becomes a purely fantastic utopia, a dangerous ideology, with consequences such that in the moment this utopia is realized a reaction will set in, namely, a negativity worse than any of the things that have been overcome. I have said at times that it is neither the biblical nor the mythical symbols of reunion—of nature with nature, of men with nature, and of men with men—which are unrealistic but that, on the contrary, those utopias are unrealistic that isolate the social sphere from nature, from individual men, from the bond with the universe, and then expect something within the human sphere that can be meaningful only if it is expected in unity with a universal healing or "making whole." I believe that the prophets with their symbols of peace within nature and peace among men as a unity were more realistic than are the pacifists and socialists who expect peace among men without peace within nature, for man after all is part of nature. And if nature itself cannot be pacified, how can peace be established within the social order? This remark does not at all mean that I would like to take the myth literally. The word "myth" protects me, I hope, from transforming symbols into objects. But we must *understand* symbols, and then we learn that myths can be more realistic than seemingly unmythical utopias that are projected into history. What appears as negative in the social order is the power structure, but power structure is necessary. Every living thing at every moment is determined by both *power and love*—that is, by standing on one's own feet, by union with another, and by the transcending unity of these two, in which power and love are simultaneously present and are held together as justice. Power cannot be conceived separately from love; for this reason all theologies, non-Christian as well as Christian, have attributed power to the gods, and in Christianity God is power and love, not merely love, as bad, sentimental theology has said. If the divine is power, power cannot be bad; in utopia, therefore, it is not the power structure of society that is denied but the *ruling structure*, which is everywhere actual as an estranged ruling structure—now, in our present, in existence after the original and before the final state of things.

The estranged ruling structure has two sides—one more inward and one more outward. The first is *authority*, the second, *exploitation*. The present social structure presupposes authority. Here I do not mean only the social structure of 1950 but also that of a hypothetical 100,000 years before and after Christ; that is, the social structure after the primordial and before the final state. Authority in turn presupposes that the individual has lost his direct relationship to the ground of being and that there are some few men or groups who are closer to this unity. This accounts for the primacy of the priesthood in all cultures, because it is assumed that priests stand nearer to the ground of being, therefore nearer to truth, and consequently have authority others are not able to have. From this follows the second, the outward, side, namely, the "use" of the masses by these few who represent authority, which in the language of sociology is called exploitation—the use of the productivity of others on the pretext that it serves the purposes (*Aufbau*) of power but in reality the purposes of the estranged ruling group. This abuse can be practiced by individuals, despots, or classes that are capable of using the situation of human existence for such authority and exploitation. The social utopia for this reason is always two-sided—it means both overcoming authority and overcoming exploitation. It is interesting that this idea runs through the whole of history. We see it in the prophecy of Joel, which has been decisive for interpreting the Pentecost event—or, rather, has been decisive for the conception of its interpretation, namely, that every individual immediately possesses the spirit of God, that servants and maidens will prophesy because the spirit of God rests immediately upon them. And this utopian prophesying is one of the foundations of all anti–authoritarian developments, for spirit is always the anti-authoritarian element in the church and is consequently regarded by the church with suspicion. From these ideas there sprang up in the Middle Ages in the celebrated utopia of Joachim di Fiore the conception of the Third Age, that of the Holy Spirit following the Age of the Father and the Age of the Son. In this Third Era every individual will live in a monastic existence and have immediate spiritual reality, and thus be independent of any hierarchy. Sociologically, the movement was a revolt of monasticism against the hierarchy. But it contains within it a profound ontological idea, the idea of immediacy: every individual is immediately related to God, he has his Spirit. This utopia became powerful in the late-Franciscan movement at the end of the thirteenth century among the so-called Spiritual Franciscans, who regarded themselves as the order in which the prophecy of Joel had been fulfilled, and who on this basis attacked the hierarchy.

The developments issuing from them gave rise to the *revolutionary bourgeois society* of the seventeenth and eighteenth centuries, which ultimately found expression in the French Revolution and in German classical thought and poetry. Everywhere in these phenomena we have the utopia of the Third Age, the age originally conceived as the Age of the Spirit, that is, of immediacy, and later as the Age of Reason.

In history the immediacy of the spirit always passes over into the immediacy of the rational structure of human consciousness, and it did so in this development. The faith in autonomy of the Enlightenment is the utopia that led from Joel through Joachim di Fiore, the Franciscans, and the sects of the Middle Ages to the

Reformation and beyond, finally, to the bourgeois revolution. Authority, in this development, has become superfluous, for it is now possible for every individual to participate immediately in Reason, and from the immediacy of his relation to Reason—or to the divine, for they are the same in the Enlightenment—arises the possibility of a democratic society, where there are no longer authorities. This evolution of utopia has an extradordinary historical significance. The anti–authoritarian thrust contained in it is part of most of us. We all understand Erich Fromm's distinction, in his writings and his practice, between rational and irrational authority, where by irrational authority he means psychological or pathological submission to existing authorities, and by rational authority he means what is taking place here at this moment, namely, that though you listen to me now you at the same time controvert me as soon as I finish speaking—otherwise it would be simply suggestion and not rational authority.

The other side of the social utopia refers to exploitation, which somehow is based on authority. Utopian thinking has developed two forms that oppose exploitation, the *political-egalitarian* and the *political-organic,* or the Stoic and Augustinian conceptions of the primordial state of man. The Stoic is egalitarian: all men are equal, all are free, all participate in original Reason. From these ideas then evolves the utopia that some day things will again be as they were in the golden age. From this form movements have issued which were able to establish themselves as democratic and egalitarian. The political-organic or Augustinian form indicates that differentiations were present even in the primordial state of things and that accordingly the organization of power must be organic, but in such a way that everyone participates in everything, as in an organism, and consequently no estranged ruling group arises. To the first form belong those ideas which lead eventually to anarchism; to the second, those which lead to organistic thinking with all its dangers of reaction and false conservatism.

Let me say a few words in addition about the *utopia of the return to the Ground* from which we are estranged. This utopia assumes different forms, for example, that of absorption in the One as it appears in certain kinds of mysticism, especially in the Indian form of Nirvana, which is by no means nonbeing but the fulfillment of individual being in the universal, the ground of being, where the individual disappears as a drop of water in the water jug. This utopia is not to be found in Christianity or in the West. I have shown that the Western and Christian utopia corresponds to an entirely different historical consciousness, that it is a utopia (as in Augustine, for instance) which brings about the restoration of unity with the ground of being, through the vision of God. Yet we remain distinct from him and indeed in such a manner that the dynamic of life is overcome through the intuitive vision—following Greek precedent. In the prophetic idea of the kingdom of God individual realities are likewise preserved; personality and community remain but as something reunited with the Ground from which they have come. Individuality is affirmed and not denied, and in this way the idea of love is made possible as a structure of eternity, for love includes both the separation and the reunion of lover and beloved. Without separation there is no reunion, and without reunion there is no love. This is the form of utopia most adequate for Christian thinking from the Jewish prophets to Protestantism; and utopia is here also the principle by which empirical realities are evaluated. This utopia is quite different from the immanental ones of the kingdom of Reason, of democracy, and of the classless (that is the nonexploitative) society. But the question that persists and the one I would like to pose at the end now is this: What about the problem of the immanental and the transcendental utopia? Or, in order to avoid these terms: What about a utopia that finds fulfillment within history and one that looks beyond history? If both must be affirmed—and I believe they must be—then how do these two forms of utopia relate to each other?

4. CRITIQUE AND JUSTIFICATION OF UTOPIA*

Let me briefly summarize for this final lecture the course of the preceding three. First, we elaborated the view that to be man means to have utopia, for utopia is rooted in the being of man itself. Second, we found that to understand history, that is, to have his-

---

* Translated by William R. Crout; revised by James L. Adams.

torical consciousness and activity, we must posit utopia at the beginning and at the end; and third, we discovered that all utopias are negations of negation—the denial of what is negative in human existence. From these bases there now can be developed that evaluation of the meaning and significance of utopia to which I wanted to lead you. This I shall do in three steps—showing first the positive meaning of utopia; second, the negative meaning; and third, the transcendence of utopia.

We begin with the *positive meaning of utopia*, and the first positive characteristic that must be stressed is its truth—utopia is *truth*. Why is it truth? Because it expresses man's essence, the inner aim of his existence; it shows what man essentially is. Every utopia is a manifestation of what man has as inner aim and what he must have for his future fulfillment as a person. I repeat an idea that perhaps was not fully understood when expressed earlier, and say that this is valid for man's personal existence just as much as for his social existence, and that it is impossible to understand the one without the other. The social utopia loses its truth if it does not at the same time fulfill the person, and the personal utopia loses its truth if it does not simultaneously bring fulfillment to society.

I illustrated this by pointing to the utopias of healing, for spiritual disorders, as current medical discussion concerning healing has extensively shown, cannot be overcome exclusively in the individual and in fulfillment of his inner meaning if society at the same time does not provide the framework within which such fulfillment can be sustained. This is revealed in the despairing statement made to me once by a neurologist and analyst. "There are men whom I have healed," he said, "but I send them back into the social structure in which we live, and I know they will return and beg for my help again." And conversely, it is impossible to understand the social apart from the personal as the inner fulfillment and inner aim of man. This is the tragedy of the revolutionary movements of the past hundred years, all of which foundered inwardly, and many outwardly, because they expected to heal society without at the same time healing individuals who are the bearers of society. Much of the tragedy of our situation is due to the fact that the utopia in the individual and the utopia in the social sphere are torn asunder and are not seen in their unity. If utopia is truth, then to deny utopia, whether in cynical or in philosophical fashion, is to negate this truth.

The second positive characteristic of utopia is its *fruitfulness*, which stands in closest relationship to its truth. Utopia opens up possibilities that would remain hidden if not seen by utopian anticipation. Every utopia is an anticipation of human fulfillment, and many things anticipated in utopias have been shown to be real possibilities. Without this anticipatory inventiveness innumerable possibilities in human history would have remained unrealized. Where no anticipating utopia opens up possibilities, there we find a decadent present, there we find that not only in individuals but also in whole cultures the self-realization of human possibilities remains stifled. Men without utopia remain sunk in the present; cultures without utopia remain imprisoned in the present and quickly fall back into the past, for the present can be fully alive only in tension between past and future.

The third positive characteristic I would like to stress is its *power* —utopia is able to transform the given. If we consider the great utopian movements, this becomes immediately evident. Judaism is perhaps the most momentous utopian movement of human history, for directly and indirectly it has elevated all mankind to another sphere of existence on the basis of its utopia of the coming reign of God. Bourgeois society with its utopia of the rational state—the Third Age of history—has revolutionized, directly or indirectly, the farthest corners of the earth and has called into question and finally made altogether impossible all pre-bourgeois forms of existence. In the same way Marxism, through its utopia of the classless society, has revolutionized and transformed directly one half of the world and indirectly the other half. In each of these three examples we encounter utopia, something that has no present because it has no place—οὐ τόπος, "without a place;" but this utopia, which is nowhere, has proved itself the greatest of all powers over the given. The root of its power—and this returns us to the first lecture—is the essential or ontological discontent of man in all directions of his being. No utopia would have power if it were exclusively economic or exclusively intellectual or exclusively religious. Nor is it true, as a false analysis would have us believe, that those who are lowest in society in terms of power of being are the real bearers of

utopia because of their discontent. Rather, the bearers of utopia are
those who in the tension between security and advancing forward
have decided for advance, and then often obtain the support of the
discontented masses, using them for the struggle even though in the
end they are swallowed up by those masses. In any case, it is an experience of history that the bearers of utopia are never those who
stand on the lowest rung of the economic ladder, whose discontent
is basically economic and nothing more. On the contrary, the
bearers of utopia are those who have sufficient power of being to
achieve advance. I think of the French revolution where the proletariat contributed indispensable assistance but where it was the
highly cultivated bourgeoisie who accomplished the revolution. One
thinks of the Franciscan revolution where it was the most advanced
forms of monasticism which revolted against the church. One thinks
of Marx's analysis of the avant-garde—those at once within the
proletariat and yet in part outside who are the real bearers of
utopia. In other words, the power of utopia is the power of man
in his wholeness. Because of his ontological discontent he is able
to push forward in all directions of being and to transform reality.
. . . So much for the positive meaning of utopia, the Yes that we
must say to it.

Now the *negative meaning of utopia*: if I previously affirmed the
truth of utopia, I now stress its *untruth*. The untruth of utopia is
that if forgets the finitude and alienation of man, it forgets that
man as finite unites being and nonbeing and that under the conditions of existence man is always estranged from his true being. For
this reason utopia in its untruth finds it impossible to lay hold of,
and thus depend on, man's true being as real. I think, for example,
of the idea of progress, an idea that, to be sure, acknowledges the
finitude of the individual, at least for this life, and often grants him
development in an afterlife. But it forgets that even in an "afterlife" finitude would make itself felt in every "moment" inasmuch as
this is a question not of eternity but of the endless continuation of
finitude.

The untruth of utopia is its false image of man, and insofar as
utopia constructs its thought and action on this untruth one can
only attack it by showing that the man it presupposes is unestranged
man. Here, however, utopia contradicts itself, for it is precisely the

utopian contention that estranged man must be brought back from his estrangement. But who will do this? Estranged man himself? Then how is estrangement overcome (*aufgehoben*)? And if someone answers, Not by man at all but by inevitable economic or other processes, then the reply must be made that the understanding of these processes is once more a human act. Even though one says that freedom is the knowledge of necessity, this knowledge stands over against nonknowing, and it must be possible to make a decision between them. But where there is a decision, there is freedom. Otherwise, the statement "Freedom is the knowledge of necessity" merely obscures and does not clarify, for it shows no understanding of what is called knowledge, namely, participation beyond necessity in truth itself or the ability to contradict truth—and this we presuppose in every moment. Here is where the untruth of utopia lies —not in its depiction of something fantastic in the future. That is unimportant, but its fundamental failure is in presupposing a false image of man contrary to its own basic assumption. For we saw that almost all utopias speak of the total estrangement and sinfulness of the present or of a social group or a people or a religion, and that they want to lead out of this situation, but they do not say how it is possible if estrangement is radical. This is the kernel of utopia's untruth, while on the other side utopia is truth.

And again I counter a positive characteristic with a negative in pointing, second, to the *unfruitfulness* of utopia, in addition to and over against its fruitfulness. The fruitfulness of utopia is its discovery of possibilities, and this can occur only by pushing forward into the limitless realm of possibilities. The unfruitfulness of utopia is that it describes impossibilities as real possibilities and fails to see them for what they are, impossibilities, or as oscillation between possibility and impossibility. In doing so it falls into pure wish-projections, which of course have something to do with what is essentially human characteristics but not with what is actually so. That is the unfruitfulness of utopia, and it is the reason theologians and also political philosophers such as Marx have rightly turned against the detailed portrayal of utopias and have made their contents dependent on possibilities that in the meantime were shown to be genuine possibilities without leaping over realities. On the other hand, they have resisted describing utopia as a fool's paradise because the fool's paradise of course is utopia for all who see activity as something negative, just as it is for those who have already fallen away from the genuinely human. And this is the origin of the fantastic quality of such utopias. They conform not to real possibilities but to fantastically exaggerated wishes for an existence that itself needs to be overcome. This is the unfruitfulness of utopia in contrast to its fruitfulness.

The third negative characteristic is the *impotence* of utopia in addition to its power. The impotence of utopia issues from the fact that for the reasons I have mentioned—that is because of its untruth and unfruitfulness—it leads inevitably to disillusionment. In order to understand it adequately, this disillusionment must be raised from the psychological to the metaphysical sphere. It is a metaphysical disillusionment that we ourselves have experienced again and again, and it is experienced so profoundly because it disturbs man in his inmost being. Such disillusionment is an inevitable consequence of confusing what is ambiguously provisional with what is unambiguously ultimate. Moving and living into the future, however, we live always in the provisional and therefore in the ambiguous, and when something preliminary is established as ultimate, disillusionment results. Two consequences arise from this which are both very destructive because of the impotence of utopia. The first is that those who are disillusioned may become fanatics against their own past. This is especially true of those— the intelligentsia above all—who at some time in their life committed themselves to a utopia not as something preliminary but as something ultimate and then had to learn not only that it was preliminary and ambiguous but also at times unequivocally demonic. This has happened to the intelligentsia in America, and objectively and humanly it is one of the saddest and most problematic experiences of American existence, as I believe it to be of Western existence generally and far beyond. This whole class of men represents today one of the most tragic groups in human society and in a certain respect one of the most dangerous because they inevitably transfer their fanaticism against themselves to everyone who does not share it and whom they therefore take to be a secret friend of those against whom their fanaticism is directed. This is one side of the matter, and perhaps it is not possible here to judge adequately the extent to which this destructiveness is effective among the intelligentsia, and even within politics.

The other side is that the utopian activists, those who still affirm the utopian goal and, while affirming it, have power to preserve it in spite of its provisional and ambiguous character, must guard against disillusionment in order to hold out—and to do so they must make use of terror. Terror is an expression of the disillusioning character of an actualized utopia; the political effects of disillusionment are staved off by means of terror.

In other words, through disillusionment and through reaction against possible disillusionment, the impotence of utopia comes to be a demonic force in society. It is just as in the physical realm and everywhere in the spiritual: an empty space never stays empty. If a demon is driven out and the space remains empty, seven new demons come to claim it; if a utopia posits something preliminary as absolute, disillusionment follows. And into this empty space of disillusionment the demons flock; today, especially here [in Germany] we find ourselves struggling with them.

This is the negative meaning of utopia, which is just as real as its positive aspect. But do not think that because I have discussed the negative characteristics after the positive that I consider the negative to have the last word. The positive remains in spite of the power of the negative, and the demand for a way beyond this negativity leads to the *transcendence of utopia*. Every living thing drives beyond itself, transcends itself. The moment in which it no longer does this, in which it remains bound within itself for the sake of internal or external securities, the moment in which it no longer seeks to take upon itself the experiment of living, in that moment it loses life. Only where life risks itself, stakes itself, and imperils itself in going as far as possible beyond itself, only there can it be won. This universal principle, this universal primal law or ontological structure of being itself, that life transcends itself although it seeks to preserve itself, that it remains within itself and seeks to protect itself in its transcending, is a structure, a principle, that is valid also for utopia. What lies beyond reality—what has not yet become reality—lies still beyond the decision of whether it is possible or impossible, and for this reason utopia is always and necessarily suspended between possibility and impossibility. If we now consider what I have said concerning the negative aspects of utopia, the question arises: Is it not possible to go beyond this whole situation in which utopia finds itself? Is it not possible to overcome its negativity by transcending not just a little but by transcending radically? And to transcend radically means not to transcend in the horizontal dimension but in the vertical—to go beyond the entire sphere of horizontal transcending. This raises the problem of whether it is possible to transcend the structure of self-preservation and self-transcendence as such—to go beyond it radically in a vertical direction, or better, in that dimension where movement is simultaneously upward and downward, out of line and plane. This is no theoretical question but one that can be pointed to in the historical evolution of culture, from which most utopias come.

If we consider the prophetic line, then we discover in the great prophets of the Old Testament a remarkable oscillation, an ambiguity, between a partial transcendence, which we can call utopia in the political and social sense, and a radical transcendence, the intrusion of something—the divine—that breaks through the entire horizontal dimension. In the prophetic texts both are present. They contain political, social, economic, and spiritual elements, and at the same time we find that these elements, which can be made intelligible from history itself, are transcended; an apocalyptic element is also present. This is the fascinating character of such descriptions as the prophet Isaiah's, for example, of peace among animals and among men, where we see a twofold intermingling and uniting of the natural and the miraculous. But like all utopias, the prophetic utopias also brought to people, anew and permanently, that metaphysical disillusionment of which I spoke, and like the disillusionment over current utopias, it also penetrates to the depths and has similarly ruinous consequences. Thus there appeared the next stage of transcendence, the one we ordinarily call apocalyptic—the visionary unveiling of something from beyond history, of something opposed to history which comes into history from "above" as a new creation. This second stage transcends the political and social elements without, however, denying them. The next stage, the third, leads on to the Christian conception of the end as it is found in the New Testament. Here social elements have disappeared altogether, and we find the heavenly kingdom that is painted in mystical colors or depicted as loving reunion with the divine. And then, finally, there is the fourth stage for which the term "utopia" can no longer be used. To it belong the mystical form of Christianity and mysticism in general; here all finite elements are extinguished by fulfillment in the beyond, which is not really fulfillment but negation.

If we look at these four stages and ask what they have meant for history, we discover that the nearer they were to the political realm the more they manifested the negative and positive characteristics of every utopia—its truth, its fruitfulness, and its power; and at the same time its untruth, unfruitfulness, and impotence. And the nearer we approach the mystical negation of every utopia, the less real are the political and the social, the less is asserted concerning man's true being, and the less danger there is of metaphysical disillusionment with all its effects.

In response someone could say: Let us then give up every utopia —let us give up not only the prophetic utopia and its secular consequences, but let us also give up the eschatological, apocalyptic utopia that still clings to the earth and its political and social realities, and let us turn to the Christian utopia in case we do not want to give ourselves over to that which is quite beyond the utopian, that is, to mystical absorption. Perhaps there are men who will go this way as a result of great metaphysical disillusionment, for history shows this way has been taken because of such disillusionment.

But if we go this way, if we elevate utopia more and more out of the horizontal into the vertical, into the transcendent, then the danger inevitably arises that the truth, fruitfulness, and power of utopia will be sacrificed. This can occur in the form of a reactionary religious conservatism that misunderstands utopia in its truth and denies it, preaching the affirmation of present realities and commitment to the present, even in political matters. Such conservatism can combine with a purely transcendental vision of human fulfillment—but it then loses power over history. We met with this sort of thing before World War I in Lutheranism where such a conservative transcendental form of utopia was set against every attempt to change reality. We found it also in certain forms of transcendental theology, which with the revelation that falls into reality from above negates every real betterment of reality. But we find it, too, in the half-religious, half-antireligious stance of certain existential-ists who reject the idea of utopia in favor of the idea of an absolute freedom of the individual, without going forward. That happens when utopia is denied, if it is not seen as true, if its fruitfulness is missed and its power thereby undermined. The consequences of this, as we know from history, are extraordinary. The religious transcendentalism that denies utopia has condemned whole peoples, the Germans in part among them, to passivity in face of action that changes history and transforms reality. The result is that in return the revolutionary-utopian forces take their stand with tremendous power and thrive in such a situation, just as they do now almost everywhere in the world, for religions at their center either are quite beyond any utopia, like the great mystical religions of the East, or have at least a transcendent utopia in which political concerns are barred. Where this is true, the aggressive utopia proves to be an almost irresistible power in the moment when convulsions of an economic, political, or spiritual kind have weakened the latent forces of resistance, and then the revolutionary utopia takes over. There we have a fragment of the analysis of a great part of human-ity in the present.

Let me in conclusion attempt briefly to formulate how we should regard utopia on the basis of its positive and negative meaning and its transcendence. The problem for my generation became a living one when we returned from World War I and found in Germany a conservative Lutheranism with its transcendental utopia in sharp conflict with utopian socialism, an exclusively immanental utopia.

Socialism had won the revolution because the forces of the con-servatives had been disorganized or destroyed by the war. In con-trast, Lutheranism, by far the Protestant majority in Germany, had adopted a contemptuous, exasperated, and negative stance toward the horizontal utopia and had reproached it for being utopian in the sense of the untruth of utopia. In this moment the problem of politics and religion ceased to be abstract for us and became concrete. From our experiences in the war and our own reflections we were certain of two things: first, that a utopia of simply going forward did not grasp the human situation in its finitude and estrangement, and that it must therefore lead necessarily to metaphysical disillusionment; and, second, that a religion for which utopia is exclusively transcendent cannot be an expression of the New Being, of which the Christian message is witness. These were the two firm points from which we proceeded, and on the basis of these two clear negations we then attempted to understand what utopia could mean in its truth, its fruitfulness, and its power if we did not fall into its untruth, unfruitfulness, and impotence, and into the metaphysical disillusionment that issues from this impotence. We answered that in the horizontal dimension something can happen, something new, something realizable here and now, under present circumstances and conditions, with the possibilities given to us, and that we must go forward in order to see these possibilities and convert them into reality. We believed it to be an "hour of fulfillment" of possibilities which earlier could not come to fulfillment. Thus we affirmed the idea of utopia. We believed that the essential nature of man demands a new order and that this new order can be born in a definite historical moment for a particular historical period. That was one side of our answer, and with it we opposed the transcendental theology of Lutheranism. On the other side we declared that this order is a preliminary and consequently ambiguous one, and that for this reason we did not dare affirm it as absolute. But then came the things that were so horrible —terror, and fanaticism turned against itself. These two things show that whenever any utopia is actualized, because it is actualized within existence it remains provisional and ambiguous. We were told that if we expressed such an idea, for which we adopted the Greek term *kairos*—the "right time," the hour of fulfillment that previously was not there and afterward no longer will be—we would weaken the revolutionary forces of the immanental utopia. For the power of a utopian movement depends on its ability to demand an unconditional faith, and if it fails to receive such faith it cannot be actualized. That was perhaps the most difficult problem in the genesis of this concept of Kairos, and one for which there is no perfect solution.

There is, however, an ultimate solution, though not a perfect one. Under certain conditions a fanaticism often arises that idolatrously sets up something finite as absolute; this possibility is always given, for when their security is at stake men value nothing more than being able to surrender themselves totally to a finite reality. When they do there then deveolps from this total submission an abundance of combative forces—the will to martyrdom, readiness to complete subordination, and above all what one might call "ideocracy," the sovereignty of an idea endowed with divine validity, even to the extent of becoming a substitute for God, no longer subject to doubt and therefore exacting unconditional adherence. This is always a possibility, and the forces that are aroused in this way dare not be underestimated. These are indeed great forces, but our question is this: Should we leave such forces alone because of this possibility of fanaticism and idolatry? Should we let them go their way? For a time they may prove more than a match for us, but the moment will come when it turns out that the question is one of finite forms that have been made absolute, and then they collide with other finite forms and in this collision are shattered. That appears to me to be an inescapable consequence, and thus we face here the problem of not using the forces of fanaticism and yet of demanding an unconditional commitment against them in the hour of necessity. In committing ourselves, however, we know that we are not committed to something absolute but to something provisional and ambiguous and that it is not to be worshiped but criticized and, if necessary, rejected; but in the moment of action we are able to say a total Yes to it. This is true not only in social life but also in every moment of our private life when we surrender ourselves to a cause or person. If we commit ourselves idolatrously, then metaphysical disillusionment is inevitable. Then the finite object or cause that has been made absolute collides with our own finite nature and shatters. But if we say Yes to something whose finitude we at the same time acknowledge, then the truth of utopia is on our side and this truth will ultimately triumph. I know how difficult this position is—I know that from the deliberations in those years between the world wars in which we were rebuked repeatedly by the utopians among us for undermining the forces of the struggle because in practice we invoked this principle of ultimate criticism. I believe that history has proved us right.

This is one answer we gave to the criticism of that time and the answer I still give today, although the concrete situation has changed vastly. The second answer concerns the relation of the transcendent and immanent utopia, or perhaps better, since these terms have so many false connotations, of the vertical and the horizontal utopia. This answer is the *idea of the two orders*, one in the horizontal plane, the order of finitude with its possibilities and impossibilities, its risks, its successes and its failures; and another, a vertical order, for which we can only use a symbolic term and which secular and religious utopias have expressed in symbols such as "kingdom of God," "kingdom of heaven," "kingdom of righteousness," and so on. Whatever the meaning of these symbols might be, it cannot be described literally because no objective concept can produce a meaningful statement about it. But we do have knowledge of this second order, because the two "orders" participate reciprocally in each other. The vertical order participates in the horizontal order—that is, the kingdom of God is actualized in historical events. It is both actualized and at the same time is resisted, suppressed, expelled. But it is this militant kingdom of God in history that cannot generate illusion because it does not promise a utopian finality to any "place" in history but makes itself known again and again in ever new realizations, so that the truth of utopia is always borne out. This reciprocal participation of the two orders is the solution to the problem of utopia. A kingdom of God that is not involved in historical events, in utopian actualization in time, is not the kingdom of God at all but at best only a mystical annihilation of everything that can be "kingdom"—namely, richness, fullness, manifoldness, individuality. And similarly, a kingdom of God that is nothing but the historical process produces that utopia of progress or revolution whose catastrophic collapse brings about metaphysical disillusionment.

In the doctrine of the two orders we have both historical reality and transhistorical fulfillment: we have the vertical, where alone fulfillment is to be found, yet precisely where we are unable to see it but can only point to it; and the horizontal, where fulfillment is realized in space and time but where just for this reason it can be found only in an anticipatory, fragmentary way—in this hour, in that form. This was our twofold answer, and here I would also like to say that all phenomena since the end of World War I, when these ideas were conceived, have proved them right, and they appear to me today to be still the solution. Whether one can speak today in the sense of a Kairos, as it was unquestionably possible to speak after World War I in Germany—and in a way that penetrated far beyond the borders of Germany—no one who is now already emerging out of that period into a new one can judge. But my own personal feeling is that today we live in a period in which the Kairos, the right time of realization, lies far ahead of us in the invisible future, and a void, an unfulfilled space, a vacuum surrounds us. But I would like to request that you take it as only a quite personal opinion that forces itself upon me when I compare with one another the situation after both world wars in Germany and in America. What is important are the principles that follow from this situation as well as from that one. In whatever way we describe the situation, what is important is the idea that overcomes utopia in its untruth and makes it manifest in its truth. Or, as I could perhaps say in summation of all four lectures on utopia: *it is the spirit of utopia that conquers utopia.*

Index

71 72 73 10 9 8 7 6 5 4 3 2 1